TAI CHI

for a healthy body, mind & spirit

TAI CHI

for a healthy body, mind & spirit

THE NI FAMILY TAI CHI TRADITION

by Hua-Ching Ni and Mao Shing Ni

with Joseph A. Miller, Ph.D.

TAO OF
WELLNESS
PRESS
Los Angeles

Published by
Tao of Wellness Press
An Imprint of SevenStar Communications
13315 W. Washington Boulevard, Suite 200
Los Angeles, CA 90066
www. taoofwellness.com

Publisher's Cataloging-in-Publication Data

Ni, Hua Ching.
     Tai chi for a healthy body, mind & spirit : the Ni family tai chi tradition
/ by Hua-Ching Ni and Mao Shing Ni ; with Joseph Miller. -- Los
Angeles : Tao of Wellness Press, 2011.

          p. ; cm.
          ISBN: 978-1-887575-31-7

     Includes bibliographical references and index.

     1. Tai chi. 2. Tai chi--Health aspects. 3. Tai chi--Psychological
aspects. 4. Spiritual life--Taoism. I. Ni, Maoshing. II. Miller, Joseph
Anthony, 1959- III. Title.

GV504 .N56 2011   2010934735
613.7/148--dc22   1101

Cover design and photographs by Justina Krakowski
Cover model: Kumiko Yamamoto, L. Ac.
Page layout and design by Meagan Brusnighan

Table of Contents

PART THREE: TAI CHI PRACTICE

PART FOUR: THE NI FAMILY TAI CHI TRADITION

Preface

It was 4:30 on a typical morning and the familiar warm hands rubbing my eyes, nose and ears made it hard to ignore and to continue sleeping. I had no choice but to wake up! My brother had the same fate and was no exception. Whenever we'd complain about the absurdly early hours, our father would explain that the energy or qi was the best before the whole city woke up. Thus began our day, as each morning we followed our father on a 20 minute walk from our house to a city park where his Tai Chi class typically began at 5 a.m. On our walks, he would instruct us to hold our hands in a fist, curl our tongue and be very quiet.

At the park, I remember vividly that there was a big banyan tree overlooking the class with its heavy, sprawling arms extending in all directions. Since we were too little to keep up with the class, our father would put us on the tree branches and instruct us to hold various poses, say "crane standing on one leg" or "tiger gathers energy and crouches" from the Eight Treasures, which is an exercise fundamental to Tai Chi, and remain still. After meeting his requirements, we were then allowed to climb, swing and chase each other all over the tree like a couple of monkeys. I remember how much I really enjoyed that part. As we grew bigger, we were brought down to the ground from the tree to join the rest of the class. But I still have fond memories of the banyan tree. Our father told us that particular banyan tree was old and wise and was generous with its "qi" or energy.

Our father also taught us the practice of "rooting," like a tree with firm foundation that is not easily uprooted—an important concept in Tai Chi. I got really good at standing in the bus without holding onto to any support, balancing between accelerations, stops and turns, all the while avoiding touching other passengers. As we practiced Tai Chi at the park, our father would ask his students to "experience the universe we are part of—the sun, moon, stars, trees, mountains in the distance, lakes in the yonder, the sea nearby, and all the myriad manifestations of the same universal essence that we also share." For many students, Tai Chi was an exercise they were looking for to help them improve their health and increase energy. For some, it was a spiritual practice that helped them connect to the vast omnipotent universal energy. For others, it helped them release their pent up emotions and expressed their feelings creatively through the movements of Tai Chi. Many martial artists also came to class because it was an essential practice to enhance and master their qi.

Long ago, humans needed a way to express their communion with the divine. During the various rituals that were devised for this purpose, ancient people performed trance-induced movements that sometimes went on for days. This was their experience of the divine universal energy and was often referred to as the "Cosmic Dance." In ancient China, the wise Tao masters recognized the spiritual value of these dances and further developed it into movements that would also benefit their health and protect them from enemies and prey. They perfected practices that would help people unite their mind, body and spirit. Thus, evolving into what we know today as Tai Chi Chuan, or Tai Chi in the West.

Growing up with the philosophy of Tao as a practical way of life was an enriching experience. The Tao is not a religion to be worshiped but a guide to a happy, healthy and harmonious life. Some later traditions of Taoism became religious but the tradition of my family — The Integral Way, remained esoteric and inwardly focused. Its teaching taught me to be open, flowing and natural at all times. The Tao also taught me "balance" as essential to flourishing through the cycles of change in life. Many of my patients have asked about the meaning of Yin and Yang, since this is the philosophy underlying the practice of Chinese health and fitness. Balance is also the key Tai Chi Principle and can easily be applied to every aspect of life. It has certainly helped me in finding fulfillment and balance in sports, work and relationships.

The simplest way to understand Yin and Yang is to look at our planet. While the northern hemisphere is basking in summer, the southern hemisphere is bundled in winter. So while Yang represents the exuberant activity of the summer, Yin represents the quiet resting of the winter. This alternating cycle of expansion and contraction occurs in all natural phenomena and is necessary for renewal of all things living. Interestingly, according to scientific theories of genesis, when the planet earth was first formed billions of years ago, it was covered in water—a vast, cold and dormant sea enveloping the whole earth. This is Yin at its purest state. Through the interaction of lightning or fire with water, the first single cell organism was formed. As the temperature rose and after volcanic eruptions and shifts in earth plates, dry land and mountains began to appear. The first single cell organism subsequently evolved into the myriad living creatures as a result of more hospitable environments. This is the action of fire and represents Yang. Without Yang, Yin remains dormant. Without Yin, Yang has nothing to develop upon. The interdependent nature of Yang and Yin, just like man and woman, are mutually beneficial.

All living organisms require a balanced alternation of activity and rest, growth and renewal—in other words, balance of Yang and Yin, respectively. Yang represents function while Yin represents form. So Form and Function must complement each other in order to become useful. Within humans, form and function can each become excessive or deficient, leading to disease, or in the context of Chinese medicine, imbalance of Yin and Yang. "Disease," my father would always say, "is a symptom of life out of balance." Tai Chi unifies the Yin and Yang in your being and brings about balance and harmony. By learning and applying the principles of Tao, you can enjoy health and longevity; not just merely survive, but thrive through life's challenges.

Today, many styles are available to a student of Tai Chi, but most of them emphasize only one aspect of its original purpose; either the martial arts or only the health perspective. The spiritual aspect has been lost. Hence, the reason for this book—to present Tai Chi as a powerful tool for cultivating the mind, body and spirit. This book intends to introduce Tai Chi as it was originally envisioned and practiced long ago by the Masters of Tao—as a tool for self-cultivation of the integration of mind, body and spirit. The styles introduced in the book came from the same Tao tradition that focuses on the three spheres of mind, body and spirit. These styles—Harmony, Gentle Path, Sky Journal and Infinite Expansion have never before been seen outside of the Integral Way Tradition. Readers will also be able to learn from the clear and concise illustrations in the book to become proficient in the intermediate, 28-Posture Form of Harmony Tai Chi.

It's been many years since those early morning Tai Chi sessions with our father. My brother and I have taught many students of Tai Chi over the last twenty-five years and our father has since retreated from worldly life. He has changed his name to OmNi and is living in remote parts of Asia. Like the sages before him, he has taken his leave after completion of his work. Having devoted his entire life to the learning and distillation of ancient wisdom for our time, he has passed on the torch of the achieved masters of our tradition to me. I am honored to continue the work, and while I will not be waking my students at 4:30 each morning, it is my hope that readers of this Tai Chi book will be awakened by its powers and be inspired to begin a lifelong journey of self-discovery and spiritual cultivation.

Dr. Mao Shing Ni, Ph.D., D.O.M., L.Ac.
Master, Ni Family Taoist Tradition

PART ONE:
INTRODUCTION, BENEFITS AND HISTORY

1 Tai Chi and Spirituality

Tai Chi: An Ancient Spiritual Tradition

Although Tai Chi Chuan is considered by some to be a martial art, in our family tradition, it is not really involved with fighting. It is actually the practice of ancient Taoist cosmology. Through the practice of Tai Chi Movement, the universal spirit (Tao) may exhibit itself, both inside and outside the body, so that one may unite with it. It is a necessary cultivation.

Let us give you a practical illustration. What a person learns, and the kind of activities he or she engages in, influences the personality. A person who studies and practices martial arts with the fighting aspect in mind tends to be more inclined toward fighting, has less self-control and is hot-tempered. Tai Chi movements are a method of balancing oneself physically, emotionally and spiritually. Gentle physical arts are a self-healing practice which can be done every day by anyone of any age in any physical condition. Our Tai Chi exercise is different from ordinary Tai Chi Chuan, because it more fully implements and emphasizes the principles contained in Lao Tzu's *Tao Te Ching* (or the Way of Life) and the *Book of Changes and the Unchanging Truth*.

We do not teach martial arts, but we sometimes mention the application of the tai chi principle in practicing them, because a physical illustration can help someone understand it better. We learned Tai Chi exercise as part of the ancient spiritual tradition, but not for fighting purposes. It is certainly an effective method of self-defense, but its essential value is that of a philosophical and spiritual practice.

Tai Chi: A Direct Path of Spiritual Achievement

Meditation or qi movement like Tai Chi does not involve deep thinking ("qi" is sometimes spelled "chi" and is pronounced like "chee"). However, a certain level of understanding can provide a good foundation for such arts. We recommend reading the *Tao Te Ching*. The words Tao Te Ching, or "guidance for the direction of universal morality and virtue," mean the same thing as wu wei, which is usually translated as "do nothing extra." Wu wei means that in meditation, your mind does not long for anything. It has, and you have, no ambition. Do not be ambitious about your meditation or your cultivation; that would disturb your mind. Do not hold any kind of worry or fear about anything. Do not be partial to anything else. For example, if you sit there and you think "I would like to see Buddha, I would like to see the Holy Mother," that is being partial.

Tai Chi movement is part of the direct path. On the direct path, people have no need for external religion, because personal spiritual truth is what the person is and does. External religion often involves conceptual duality or dependence on a final judgement from someone else. This can cause problems in one's life and development. The direct path transcends religious beliefs. All faiths, when they reach the non-conceptual level, embody the integral truth.

People with truthful attitudes are always seeking to improve themselves. The language of each region in the world may be different, but the purpose of all languages is to serve the substance of life. Likewise, the purpose of all rituals and ceremonies is enlightenment. People may arrive at the mountain top from different directions, but once they are at the top, they all enjoy the same panoramic view.

In daily life, we like to be able to be receptive, flexible, impartial, mature, responsible, responsive, and non-glaring. Non-glare is like a translucent glass or mirror instead of a direct, blinding light. The martial arts can show off a person's talent or physical force, but in Tai Chi movement and in a spiritual life, we prefer to be non-glaring. There is a proverb here in the West that says, "Everything that glitters is not gold." In its natural state, gold ore does not shine, but there is a glittery mineral called "Fool's Gold." We could also say that we like to be "non-glittery."

Your spiritual achievement depends on what you do, your level of understanding, how much you delve into it, and how much you receive from the achievement. Although there are different levels of spiritual achievement, can you ever decide that what you have achieved is completely true and final? Spiritual achievement is the unending personal opportunity to reach the ultimate truth. In spirit as well as body, the same basic principle applies: keep moving.

Tai Chi, Energy Refinement, and the Spiritual Process

In spiritual cultivation, it is necessary to become aware of the existence of qi (energy). Ordinarily, people's nervous systems are not sensitive enough to feel the qi that is either within their own bodies or outside of them. The energy within the human body exists in four states and is constantly changing from one phase of evolution to another. The four states are: solid, as bone and tissue; liquid, as blood, lymph, etc.; the vaporized or gas state; and the electrical state, which usually occurs in sexuality. All four states have both healthy and unhealthy manifestations.

When all of these states evolve and harmonize as one integrated and undifferentiated manifestation of energy, the ancient achieved ones refer to this as "qi". Qi is invisible, but through the phenomena of life and death, its coming and going can be observed. Through the practice of Tai Chi movement, an individual can develop his sensitivity so that he may experience and control the energy within the channel system of the body (see Chapter 8).

The spiritual process is essentially a process of refining one's energy to subtler and subtler states. Tai Chi movement functions as a method by which this refinement may be accomplished so as to actualize the spiritualization of one's being. The Taoist Masters, or ancient achieved ones of antiquity, exposed the fact that there are steps comprising the process of spiritualization, which include the refinement of physical essence or sexual energy (jing) into mental energy (qi), the refinement of mental energy into spiritual energy (Shen)[1], and the refinement of spiritual energy in order to unite oneself with the Subtle Origin of the Universe (Tao), which constitutes the birth of an individual into the Immortal Realm. Tai Chi gentle exercise is a practical approach to achieving this goal.

Tai Chi and the Four Steps to Spiritual Immortality

When you do gentle movement, you are moving, yet at the same time you experience quietude, inner stillness, calmness and composure. Gentle movement combines all good spiritual virtues with the benefit of physical exercise. This great harmonization became gentle movement or Tai Chi movement.

Now we would like to talk about the position of Gentle Movement or internal energy movement in spiritual self-cultivation, spiritual self-integration or subtle self-integration of a new life. We have already explained to you that there are steps to achieving spiritual immortality. The first step is to refine one's general nutrition from food or air to become one's physical essence. This physical essence is sexual energy, because people have an animal foundation in their beingness. Sexual energy, in our terms, is called "jing." So one's sexual energy is nurtured by the food one eats and one's breathing.

The second step is to refine the sexual energy to be a higher sphere of energy called "qi." Many people do not understand qi; we will talk about it below because it is so important.

The third step is to take the qi and refine it to a higher, more subtle energy called "Shen" in Chinese.

The fourth and final step is to gather the Shen; from this gathering, a spiritual conception is accomplished. This spiritual conception is your new life. We call it a "red baby" as an analogy of a newborn baby whose skin is still pink or red. The energy of this newly created immortal life is symbolized by the newness of a human baby.

All these steps are important and constitute the internal alchemy system (referring to energy transformation) of spiritual development.[2] Perhaps the middle part, of refining sexual energy into spiritual energy, and then changing the spiritual energy into the new life are the most challenging. Why? Because they require self-control over different aspects of your being. Sometimes it seems as though you are giving something up, although you are really gaining something.

My personal experience of Tai Chi practice is that when combined with other instruction, it can take you step by step toward the goal of immortality. The practice of Gentle Movement can be useful in all the steps. By the way, during the second stage of refining one's energy toward immortal life, not only does a person refine his sexual energy into qi, one's sexual energy, mental energy and physical energy all integrate through Tai Chi or Qigong (Chi Kung) practice to become qi.

We have mentioned the steps or realistic way to achieve immortality. The place of difficulty for many people is this part. It is not hard to learn a system and transfer one's sexual energy into qi, but it is hard to maintain qi to become Shen. Shen is much more subtle. You can find the way to nurture it in the *Tao Te Ching*.[3]

So many Tai Chi or Qigong teachers are in a stage where their qi is very strong, but they use it, for example, in sex or fighting. If they do not waste their qi in sexual recreation or fighting, then in their push hands movement, a gentle touch from them can make a strong man lose his balance and fall four or five yards away. How can the person have such a power? It is not physical force; it is the gathering of qi that can do that.

Many people who practice Tai Chi or Qigong regularly and do not go deeply into understanding it use their accumulated energy in two spheres: either sex or push hands fighting. Other people, if they accumulate some energy, will discharge it in other ways – for example, in emotional outbursts. But if the person is a student of the Integral Way and is really seriously looking for spiritual immortality, he will not stay in the stage characterized by, "As a Tai Chi practitioner, I am strong in fighting or in sex. That is all I need." The serious student goes from this step and utilizes his achieved qi and refines it into Shen or spiritual energy.

Step by step, the possibility is there for immortality, so now we are releasing this secret to people who are learning. It is not hard to achieve spiritual immortality, it is hard to go through the checkpoint entitled "general sexual desire." If you stand there and do not pass, you are locked out from the sphere of spiritual immortality.

The Ni Family Spiritual Tai Chi Tradition

The Ni Family Tradition of Taoist Tai Chi includes four styles that relate to the steps of spiritual development described above. These four styles are called Harmony Tai Chi, Gentle Path Tai Chi, Sky Journey Tai Chi, and Infinite Expansion Tai Chi. The many valuable skills and helpful knowledge that we teach were not necessarily the invention of our direct ancestors. However, they learned them, preserved them and included them in our family tradition, and passed them down to benefit other people. This is the principle of our family.

The first style, "Harmony Tai Chi" (a.k.a. "Internal Harmony Style", or "Trinity Style"), captures the essence of Yang, Chen, and Wu styles. Harmony Tai Chi emphasizes balancing and refining the energy of the three energy centers of the body (the lower, middle, and upper tan tiens). Thus, it can save the serious student from having to learn the different styles separately for the purpose of health and spiritual cultivation. There is a beginner's 18-Step form, an intermediate 28-Step form, and the advanced long form consisting of 108 postures or movements. In addition, there are push hands and a number of Tai Chi instrument/weapon forms.

The second style in our tradition is "Gentle Path Tai Chi" (a.k.a. "Style of Wisdom," or the "Earth Style") which concentrates energy in the lower tan tien below the navel. This style corresponds with the physical plane. The popular Yang style exemplifies the same principle as the Earth Style; however, the original Earth Style is the genuine expression of the principle. This style refines the energy from the food we eat and the air we breathe and transforms it into physical essence (jing). The Earth Style is suitable to be performed by either the beginner or the long-trained practitioner as a means of energy adjustment. This style is appropriate for spring or summer. The spring especially is a wonderful time to gather the warmth radiated from the earth.

The third style is called "Sky Journey Tai Chi" (a.k.a. "Style of Harmony with People," the "Mankind Style"). The more ancient Chen style exemplifies the same principle as Sky Journey Tai Chi. In this style the energy corresponds with the mental plane and is concentrated in the middle tan tien. This style is suitable to be practiced in the autumn.

The fourth style is "Infinite Expansion Tai Chi" (a.k.a. "Style of Integration," or the "Heaven Style") which concentrates energy in the general yang channel in the back and neck. This is the ancient esoteric style and artful training to attune one's metabolism and rejuvenate one's internal secretions. In this style, the spirit centers the whole constitution of the being. This style accelerates the circulation, bodily secretions and excretion of toxins. It helps the metabolism of people of all ages, especially after middle age. However, quite a bit of training is required because it is the most difficult style to learn well. It is preferable that one begins to learn this style when one is young and the body is supple.

Through these styles of Tai Chi one can understand the body, mind and spirit, and bring about their reintegration. However, if one does not learn or develop the internal alchemy systems of these forms, they remain merely a superficial shell. Until just one generation ago, the internal methods of Tai Chi movement were carefully guarded secrets, the essence of natural spiritual culture. These secrets were passed only through family heritage or esoteric traditions. With much devotion, and under strict and precise instruction, one may learn and master Tai Chi movement and benefit from this treasure of spiritual culture.

2 Tai Chi: A Way to Find Spiritual Independence

[The following chapter is adapted from an article written by Marvin Smalheiser which appeared in the June, 1989 issue of *Tai Chi Magazine* and is reprinted here with permission.]

Spiritual Sufficiency

For many Westerners, Taoism seems clouded in mysticism and further obscured by contradictions that cloak as well as reveal its profound meanings. Something is there, but it is often just beyond your grasp. And yet that, too, is part of the attraction. The confusion is magnified by the cultural differences between Taoism and Western religions which can often lead to people approaching Taoism with incorrect attitudes.

As an heir to 74 generations of Taoist masters in China, Taoism is much simpler for me (OmNi). In fact, the majority of my work in the West has been advising people on how to simplify, understand and enrich their lives. Through this understanding, their lives can be integrated.

I am in my 80s now, and in my 12 years living in the United States I have established a college in Los Angeles in addition to writing many books.

Previously, my life in Taiwan included martial arts and acupuncture in addition to my spiritual teaching and writing. These careers contributed to another primary focus of mine: internal development, particularly that which increases spiritual sufficiency. This usually involves awakening people to their own sufficiency.

To become a good student of the Tao, what you need to learn is to be internally sufficient, to become internally rich, and to become bigger in ways that will help you in whatever you do.

The main goal of learning the Tao is to learn that you are internally spiritually sufficient instead of spiritually insufficient. You learn your spiritual independence instead of remaining dependent.

Once you have an understanding of Taoism, you will see that there is no disagreement with any religious sect or group.

Tai Chi Teaches Spiritual Principles

Tai Chi Chuan is one of the best ways to develop an understanding of Taoist principles because it embodies many of its most important principles: naturalness, balance, poise, symmetry and harmony. Tai Chi Chuan can be preferable to sitting in meditation, especially for those who prefer not to sit still for long periods of time.

Additionally, the transition between static meditation and our daily lives can be difficult for some people. As an example, after a period of prolonged meditation a person may not immediately feel comfortable driving a car. You may need time to adjust because these two activities require you to operate on two very different levels of life.

Tai Chi Chuan is one way you can live a good, practical life. It is a good approach to internally and externally harmonizing yourself. It can change your personal attitudes, change your moods, and change your emotional well-being.

In Tai Chi Chuan and in Taoism, you learn the same basic principles: naturalness, balance, poise, symmetry, and harmony. All the great principles are easy. They can guide your life. In Tai Chi Chuan all your learning is in one piece. What you do with your whole being, your whole learning, comes from your Tai Chi practice.

Tai Chi and Internal Harmony

Many diseases are the result of disharmony between organs or in the nervous system. If you become capable in Tai Chi Chuan, you will know how to harmonize yourself. You will know how to get rid of internal conflicts and problems. Also, by improving yourself internally, you can improve your outward defense. You will not be as impulsive or aggressive.

Deepen Your Practice Through Spiritual Study

To enrich Tai Chi Chuan practice, I suggest that in addition to learning from a teacher, students also expand their practice by studying the *I Ching, or Book of Changes*[1] and the *Tao Te Ching*.[2] By developing an understanding of the theory, students can put all their understanding into their Tai Chi practice.

This kind of Tai Chi practice has benefits over academic studies in regular schools and colleges. For example, if you go to school, you will learn many things that may not necessarily be of use in your life except to make money or do some kind of service. But if you learn Tai Chi Chuan, Taoism, the *I Ching*, and study the *Tao Te Ching*, it is certain that once you study them, everything will express itself into your Tai Chi Chuan.

This is wonderful. This makes it the embodiment of realization of Tao as well as the principle of balance, the principle of symmetry, and the principle of internal and external harmony. This can be seen directly in your Tai Chi Chuan practice.

The Best Kind of Practice

The best kind of practice – Tai Chi Chuan or Taoism – is one that lets the energy flow naturally. Many people practice methods that push the qi to circulate unnaturally in orbits, but qi circulates naturally. If you try to force it then it may cause health problems, such as making the qi to rush to the head, which can produce high blood pressure.

It is better to follow the principle of naturalness in Tai Chi Chuan. People wish to become highly achieved overnight, but this will surely cause trouble.

It is against the principle of Tai Chi.

Integrating Your Energies

In the development of Taoism there are different stages of life. We think of human life as the confluence of spiritual energy and physical energy. Usually, when we talk about heaven, we talk about spiritual energy, or universal religion. Usually, when we talk about earth, we talk about physical energy. Human life is a different category. To make it blossom, it is necessary to integrate the various energies. From this foundation, you can achieve a truly godly life.

Integrating is important. In general, people will say they are separated from their work, family, or society. Some people might have a good mind, but a good mind is not always related to a good spirit. This is because the spirit is at a higher level than the mind and the mind usually does not know the spirit.

Sometimes we make a mistake that some part of our body recognizes even before the mind knows its mistake. The mind is a student. It needs to learn and to experience difficulty. It needs to experience mistakes before it knows.

But spiritually, you don't need experience. The spirit knows already. This is why it is important for us to make a connection between the two, to look for oneness between our spiritual level and our mind's level.

I teach Taoism to promote spiritual awakening. When you awaken spiritually you can manage your life without restriction, at least without moral problems. We don't say how smart you will be. Smart is your mind. But moral trouble is a spiritual problem.

The Process of Understanding

I do not mandate strict disciplines for people trying to reach an understanding of Taoism. At first, I usually don't require discipline at all. Once you see the value, you will do it by yourself. It makes it simple. Smokers only stop when they begin to understand the trouble it causes. We don't believe in imposing discipline, personally.

Through my talks and writing I have tried to create understanding. Once you understand, then everything will come along. If you don't truly understand and only rely on the teacher to impose discipline on you, even the good discipline is going to be like a poison.

The process of reaching understanding is a gradual one, in which people may read my books and then re-read them many times to reach deeper and deeper levels of understanding.

Since I do not give extra discipline, a new student relies on their understanding of what life is about, what a good life is and how they can make improvements. It takes time. It does not work as quickly as Western medicine. It works slowly.

Fifty years ago, I didn't think I could find a friend. But now I have so many, many friends and students who enjoy the new opportunity for their own development. But it did not happen overnight.

Usually, I speak about the integral truth. It is a system built in each individual life so many people can agree with me. It is not an external thing that may apply only to Chinese culture. The truth is internal; in each individual. So when they read my books, if the channel is already open, it is very easy. That is what I am looking for. This is what I know myself. So they don't find any separation between the reading and themselves.

Spiritualize Your Life

My advice for applying Taoist practice to life is to simplify life. When it comes to spiritualizing one's life, it is also a matter of understanding. Once you fully spiritualize your life, you don't need to rely on your physical form at all. That's what we call immortality. But that will take too long for most people. For the general people, I avoid talking about it. I say live well, be happy in your life, don't cause any conflict with other people and maintain your moral standard in all your activities.

People are becoming more aware of their environment and the materialization of life. I think people will be more careful. They can see how foolish they were to create so much trouble.

People are now materialistic but this can change through the Taoist approach. In Taoist teaching we say that either you are the master or materialism is the master. If you are enslaved by material things, then you are not achieved. It is not a happy life.

In the famous painting of Lao-tzu riding on the buffalo, the buffalo represents the world or the material world. The buffalo also signifies animal desires. For most people, the buffalo would actually be riding on their heads and shoulders.

Lao-tzu was an achieved person. He rode on the buffalo and enjoyed his trip through the worldly life. Generally, the buffalo rides on people and they are pressed down by the material life.

Everyone has to pay the price for living in this world. We are looking for balance. We are looking for spiritual development. We also need to pay our bills, but your whole life energy should not become devoted to materialism.

Balancing East and West

It is turning around. There is hope. Take the example of Tai Chi movement. If we arrange our life as an extended series of Tai Chi movements, I think it will become much smoother, much happier and our general life will have fewer obstacles.

I appreciate both the Eastern and Western minds. The Western mind mostly puts its energy outward and it truly brings some improvement, such as scientific technology, political democracy and free economic activity.

But, based on my personal contacts, I believe that the Western mind has also left the internal life messy. The Eastern people, through long generations' work, have worked harder to improve the internal side, but they have left out the external life. If both minds can match together we can make internal and external improvements and not leave any side out.

The Western mind comes out of the dominance of religion looking for light so they have intelligent life, but it can also include moral improvement. You see people with developed intellect but not necessarily good moral conditions. Something is wrong there. A person's intellectual development can also influence their moral development.

A Tradition of Spiritual Sobriety

People who come to me often have the impression that I give religious teachings. But what I do is entirely different. Religion usually promotes a type of intoxication; an emotional, religious intoxication that causes people to block out rational development and fail to know the true power of the life of the world. But in the teaching of Taoism, it is completely different. It promotes spiritual sobriety, not intoxication.

My family in China had many traditions. I was born in Wenchuw, Southern Chekiang Province, near Shanghai and my tradition continues from the Tien Tai Mountain. Both my father and grandfather were doctors.

My training was mostly from my family, my father and my mother. My father had a good relationship among the masters in the Taoist Temples in the mountains, so I stayed with them in the mountain caves and temples to learn the different ways.

My training in Chinese Medicine and Taoism started when I was 10. Gradually, I left my family to develop my own practice as a healer and began traveling everywhere.

In 1949, I went to Taiwan, still relatively young. I maintained my acupuncture practice and also became a spiritual teacher. I remained in Taiwan for 27 years before coming to the United States. Now I write, travel, speak, and assist the practice of my two sons at the Tao of Wellness and Yo San University in Los Angeles.

3 A Discussion of Tai Chi Movement

Tai Chi: A Form of Qigong or Dao-In

Qigong is a general name for all kinds of gentle movement, both internal and external, that directly activate or help guide a smooth flow of qi throughout the body by use of the breath, simple movements, posture, and mental imagery. By releasing tension and stimulating vitality, the practice of Qigong promotes self-healing and strengthens the immune system. Some forms are a complete set of different movements, while others are just one or more simple movements. Each movement has a different effect.

Qigong means "energy generating." Tai Chi Chuan, or Tai Chi movement, is a form of Qigong. In general, Qigong is usually much simpler than Tai Chi. Although it is more advanced and more organized in all respects, if you were to dissect Tai Chi piece by piece, you would have Qigong. When you "move the clouds" or do a movement by itself, it is called Qigong. It is actually nothing more than semantics. Tai Chi consists of many Qigong movements that are arranged according to the principles of the *Tao Te Ching* and the *I Ching*. Different levels of practice all come from this common foundation.

Both of these arts originally developed from movement practices called Dao-In[1], which I translate as "energy conducting." Dao-In is a set of simple movements that are combined with breathing exercises. Later, because of external demands, these movements became more martial in nature. It is always easier to promote fighting skills than internal cultivation. Now that people have more understanding and development, they are coming back to the Qigong type of movement.

The Purpose and Development of Tai Chi

The original purpose of Dao-In (energy conductance exercise) was not only to exercise the body, but as life became more complicated Dao-In entered a new phase that eventually developed into martial arts, from which Tai Chi movement developed. Tai Chi is only 600 to 1,000 years old, but it is different from ordinary martial arts, because it maintains the original form of Dao-In. Some wise teachers united martial arts with Dao-In movements. The Chen Style is more of a martial art, but the Yang Style is closer to Dao-In. Although the Chen Style is older than the Yang Style, martial arts only serve a specific type of circumstance, whereas Dao-In serves everyday life.

There were also movements that preceded both the Chen and Yang Styles of Tai Chi movement, but because most people are not acquainted with ancient movements, we cannot use them as a background to discuss our own knowledge with you.

Tai Chi movement arose out of necessity, when human life arrived at a new stage. Achieved people enjoy ancient wisdom, but they also realize the need to guard themselves, not only from attack by other people, but also from animals and other natural dangers. To effectively protect oneself, spiritual, mental and physical development are all necessary. None of them can be neglected. Tai Chi responded to the need for development in all three spheres of one's being.

Tai Chi: A Tool to Develop Your Life

Because the ancient developed ones, and even those of later times, knew the value of Dao-In, they adapted this treasure of ancient development when facing new circumstances. All Tai Chi students should know that it can be either a combative activity or a civilizing influence for personal development. Its use depends on the teacher. If the teacher has more cultural depth, he will place more emphasis on the Dao-In. People of less depth, with more achievement in the physical sphere or combat, will place the emphasis on Tai Chi as a martial art. As a martial art, it is certainly an excellent achievement, but martial arts are limited. Dao-In has a greater value because it is unlimited. We value Tai Chi movement as a way to adjust physical, mental and emotional stagnation. As a practice, it is a fulfillment of the cosmology of Tai Chi.

We believe that most of you choose Tai Chi movement as a method to help your bodies and improve your health. We do not think that you use it as a fighting skill. Using Tai Chi as a tool to develop your life being is the direction of our wise ancestors who originally developed it. This is the traditional direction that does not come from fighting.

Today, our life activities are distributed or divided up in an extreme way. If you do physical work, usually you are physically active. When you do mental work, your mind is active. In most kinds of work, seldom can you link your mind and body together. Tai Chi is a special practice that can help you reunite your mind and body.

Tai Chi movements are usually done slowly. If a healthy person, say before the age of 40, learns Tai Chi just to benefit his health or for a physical purpose only, its effectiveness would be hard to see. It would be easier to see the benefits of the Eight Treasures[2]. This does not imply that Tai Chi is unnecessary or is less beneficial than the Eight Treasures. They are different forms of the same art. The reasons for practicing Tai Chi, as compared to Eight Treasures, is to augment the benefit.

Tai Chi and The Way (Tao)

The teaching of Tao values the body as a tool that can accomplish good things. Many other traditions and religions regard the body as a nuisance. Lao Tzu mentioned in the *Tao Te Ching* that the body becomes a burden when you cannot manage it.

Much of Lao Tzu's teaching is not understood or accepted by most people. For instance, his statements that the weak can conquer the strong, and that one who is still can surpass one who moves fast. Such things can be proven by the practice of Tai Chi movement. Qigong, Tai Chi and push hands are not for fighting, but are an opportunity for your body, mind and spirit to connect.

Tai Chi movement is only one step in learning Tao, it is not a place to stop, unless you enjoy fighting like a rooster or a bull. In our classes, we first teach single, simple movements like those of the Eight Treasures. When a student achieves that, then we teach them Tai Chi movement. The goal of our teaching, however, is not to train people in martial arts, but to teach them the truth contained in the *Tao Te Ching*, which is much more valuable and profound than physical movement[3].

Tai Chi and Energy (Qi) Control

Everyone breathes, but not everyone knows how to control their breath to produce more energy. Everyone also has qi (pronounced "chee"), but not everyone knows about it. Qi can be translated as breath, air or energy. It is only through certain training and cultivation that you learn about the existence of qi, or internal energy, in your own life being. After learning Tai Chi, a person could use four ounces of strength to manage a thousand pounds. This is an internal achievement that surpasses general physical strength. At the physical level alone, only a greater amount of strength can beat a lesser amount of strength, but with Tai Chi one learns to manage qi in all kinds of situations.

One important principle of Tai Chi movement is called "in ching lo kung," which means to conduct the force of one's opponent to an empty space instead of fighting it. For example, if someone is about to attack you, you subtly and gently guide him into an empty space so that he defeats himself. This is the kind of energy management that was achieved by many famed masters of Tai Chi. If the movement is simple, qi can easily be controlled. If the movement is too complicated, it is hard for beginners to control the qi. This is why we recommend learning some qigong in the beginning.

Tai Chi movement involves the expansion and contraction of energy: projecting energy and collecting it. These two sides of any activity are called yin and yang. Tai Chi brings the two forces together in your being, like a husband and wife.

Learning Tai Chi

To learn Tai Chi requires discipline. Some students may practice for several years without any apparent results, but they do not notice that now they rarely catch a cold and that other small problems have cleared up. Their whole being becomes stronger in addition to their physical strength increasing. You may not feel your energy increasing, but if you do something that decreases or hurts your energy, you immediately know it, because you feel it. For example, if you have too much sex or you play card games all night long, then the next day you will feel that you have hurt your energy. Sometimes a student of Tai Chi seems to be more affected by things than people who do jogging or general exercise. Tai Chi movement is a gentle path. It is not like going to the gym and watching your muscles develop. Ordinary physical exercise does not use your conscious mind, but with Tai Chi or qigong you must use your conscious mind to connect each movement with the next so that when the mind moves, the body moves: both in the same direction.

The Way is simple. It is not hard to learn. It is hard to keep doing and practicing it. It is hard because sometimes the mind becomes wild and rejects simplicity. Once the mind becomes complicated, you are tempted to give up and fall back into an undeveloped stage of being. You only need to learn it right, do it right and keep doing it. It has a tremendous effect on your entire life.

Tai Chi: Internal and External Harmonization

Tai Chi Movement has many benefits. For example, if people spend a lot of time doing quiet sitting or meditation, they may have difficulty driving on the freeway. Meditation and worldly life are two entirely different levels of life. Tai Chi exercise is mid-way between the two; you can still live a general, practical life.

Practicing Tai Chi movement is also a good approach to internal and external harmonization. It changes your personal attitudes, mood and personal emotion. For example, many diseases are caused by a disharmony between the organs or in the nervous system. If you practice Tai Chi movement, in time you learn how to harmonize yourself and eliminate internal conflict. Also, by improving yourself internally, your approach to the outer world will not be so impulsive or aggressive, which only provokes the environment to fight back.

No religion can serve you better than simple, nonverbal practices. You may find some consolation from religion, but true health comes from good practices. Do not fool yourself, like a donkey following a carrot on a stick. You can put a real carrot in your hand rather than watch it hanging on a stick in front of you.

4 The Benefits of Tai Chi Chuan

Tai Chi and Medical Research

In the past few years, there has been a tremendous amount of western scientific medical research on the benefits of Tai Chi. For example, a recent randomized controlled study of early postmenopausal women published in the *Archives of Physical Medicine and Rehabilitation* showed that Tai Chi practiced for 45 minutes a day for 5 days a week over a 12 month period resulted in slowing of bone loss in weight bearing bones (Chan et al., 2004). This study recommended long-term follow-up to substantiate the role of Tai Chi in the possible prevention of osteoporosis and related fractures. Another randomized controlled study published in the *Journal of Alternative and Complementary Medicine* demonstrated that Tai Chi practiced for 30 minutes a day (with a 10 minute warm and 10 minute cool-down), 3 times a week for 12 weeks resulted in decreased blood pressure, favorable lipid profile changes, and improved anxiety status in healthy subjects (Tsai et al., 2003). A third randomized controlled study, published in the *Journal of the American Geriatric Society*, showed that Tai Chi practiced for 60 minutes a day, 3 times a week over 24 weeks resulted in improved self-rated sleep quality and thus appears to be an effective, non-pharmacological sleep enhancement therapy for sleep-disturbed elderly individuals (Li et al., 2004). A fourth study, published in the *Journal of Applied Nursing Research*, reported the results of a clinical trial that demonstrated that Tai Chi practiced for 30 minutes a day, two times a week for 3 months resulted in statistically significant improvements in functional mobility, balance, and a reduction in fear of falling in older women living in retirement communities (Taggart, 2002).

There are numerous other studies showing the benefits of Tai Chi such as: (1) as a possible adjunct to cardiac rehabilitation exercise training (Taylor-Pilaie, 2003; Chao et al., 2002), (2) improvements in symptom management and quality of life for those with fibromyalgia (Taggart, et al., 2003), (4) improvements in leg muscle strength (Christou et al., 2003), (5) increased immunity to the shingles virus (Irwin et al., 2003), (6) decreased blood pressure (Thornton et al., 2004), (7) increased sense of balance, postural sway, and reduction of falls (e.g., see Tsang et al., 2004; Thornton et al.; 2004, Wolf et al., 1996; Wu et al., 2002), (8) improved joint sense (Tsang and Hui-Chan, 2003; 2004), and (9) enhanced microcirculation (Wang et al., 2001), among others. From this brief summary of recent medical research, it is clear that many of the health benefits of practicing Tai Chi known to the East are now being increasingly substantiated by Western science. See the Bibliography for suggested reading related to Tai Chi and medical research.

Self-Healing

Tai Chi movement is a self-healing method which can be practiced by anyone of any age in any condition of health. The therapeutic value of energy guidance exercise, which has had various names, has been recognized in China for thousands of years, but it is only recently that Tai Chi movement has been acknowledged in the West as a means of restoring both physical and mental health. Consistent practice of Tai Chi movement rectifies one's internal energies so effectively that the indirect result in many cases has been the curing of a wide variety of diseases, ranging from high blood pressure and ulcers to tuberculosis and heart disease. Its greatest health significance is its effectiveness in preventing disease by keeping the internal energies in a state of balance.

According to ancient integral medical theory, disease is the manifestation of energy disorder and aberration within the body. It is a state in which the various organs and the nervous system are functioning incorrectly or inadequately in a manner which is either too slow or fast, too weak or strong. When the energy flows through the channels unimpeded and the various organs are in a state of equilibrium, one is healthy. If the energy becomes imbalanced or blocked, disease manifests. Disease indicates that the energy flow needs to be corrected. Through the calmness and relaxation generated by Tai Chi movement, the vitality which has been locked within a tense and imbalanced body is released and allowed to restore and sustain natural health.

From a different perspective, disease also occurs when the mind and body are out of harmony. The activity of the mind directly affects the dynamic processes taking place within the channel system (see Chapter 8), which in turn influences the physical form. The flow of energy within the body is influenced by the thoughts one thinks and the emotions one experiences. In order for the body and organs to function in optimum health, it is necessary for the emotions to shift from one to another throughout the day, and for the stream of thoughts to flow unimpeded.

If one particular emotion or mode of thinking is habitually emphasized, a particular organ may become over stimulated, causing depletion, imbalance and blockage within the channel system. Energy flows thus become altered or impeded, and certain organs may become congested with blood and qi while others receive an inadequate supply. This results in disease. The movements of Tai Chi guide one's internal energies throughout the channels in such a way that a balance and order may be restored within the body.

The energy flow within the body is also influenced by the fact that when people are engaged in a physical activity, their minds are engaged in an unrelated activity. The mental and physical energies do not join forces, so to speak, to perform a particular task, but instead go off in different directions. This dichotomy is not the way nature intended the human organism to function, and this, too, causes energy disorder within the body.

The practice of Tai Chi movement trains the mind to follow every detail of the body's actions. In this way, rather than literally scattering energy through unmindful physical activity, one is able to gather energy into one's organism. The peaceful mental atmosphere created by Tai Chi movement allows negative thought patterns to dissolve and be replaced by positive, life-enforcing attitudes.

Tai Chi and Energy Absorption and Utilization

Tai Chi movement helps the body absorb and utilize the energy from the food we eat. Tai Chi movement accelerates the speed of energy generation within the body by producing gentle internal heat. This heat vaporizes the liquid energy derived from food in much the same way that the hot sun evaporates moisture from the earth. Because the energy from the food we eat is thus transformed from the liquid state to a vapor, it is much more easily transported and distributed to all of the organs of the body.

The human body can be likened to a tree. If the energy circulates to all parts of the tree, the entire tree is full of life. However, if one part of the tree does not receive its supply of energy, then that part withers.

Rejuvenation

In the human body, the energy must always be regenerated and it must be able to circulate freely to all parts of the body. In ordinary exercise, circulation is stimulated but energy is also burned up and lost in perspiration. Thus, one may generate energy but one also loses energy. In Tai Chi movement the body may blossom in perfect condition without causing any perspiration. One's muscle tissue will be neither flaccid nor rigid, but full of energy like a ripe peach.

Through the burning and exhaustion of energy in daily activities, people grow old very fast. Energy conducting exercise is a means of refreshing one's energy and rejuvenating one's body. There are points within the body where energy is cultivated by practitioners of spiritual arts for the purpose of regeneration and rejuvenation. In man, the general point is located in the prostrate gland and in women it is located in the thymus gland. The valley formed between the two buttocks in the case of men, and between the two breasts in the case of women, provides a natural focal point for the gathering of energy. The testicles or ovaries, the thymus and the pineal gland are the three areas most concerned with self-cultivation and correspond with the lower, middle and upper tan tien, respectively.

Tai Chi Compared to Ordinary Exercise

Ordinary exercise and sports may produce quick and shallow breathing which will cause more oxygen to enter the system. However, this type of exercise strains the heart and the lungs. In Tai Chi movement, the heart is relaxed and the breathing is deep and full. This enables even more oxygen to enter the blood stream and utilizes the full capacity of the lungs. The rythmic movements of Tai Chi exercise produce friction between the organs, causing gentle warmth which strengthens and tonifies them.

Some forms of exercise will mobilize only a particular group of muscles, while Tai Chi movement brings all of the muscles of the body into play. Tai Chi movement influences and benefits all systems of the body, in particular, the central nervous system, digestive system, respiratory system and endocrine system. The central nervous system extends from the base of the spine to the brain and is the most important system of the body. The function of the central nervous system is to receive information from both outside and inside of the body and transmit the body's actions and reactions to the brain. Through the practice of Tai Chi movement, the central nervous system is gradually strengthened, developed and refined.

Tai Chi and Internal Systems and Organs

By training the mind and the body to be calm and relaxed, the brain and central nervous system may receive and transmit information more accurately and thoroughly. In Tai Chi movement, the spine is always kept flexible and erect to allow the central nervous system to function effectively. When the spinal column is erect, blood and vital energy can be transmitted from the lower part of the body to the brain.

The expanding and contracting movements of Tai Chi gentle exercise invigorate and tone the stomach and intestines, promoting good digestion. This expansion and contraction uses the full capacity of the lungs, strengthening the entire respiratory system. The deep and rhythmic breathing which is an intrinsic aspect of Tai Chi movement causes the diaphragm to massage the internal organs and aids the circulation of fresh blood to the viscera. The circulation of fresh blood promotes the proper functioning of the endocrine system, which restores the chemical balance of the body. When the chemical balance of the body becomes rectified, metabolism improves.

Energy Adjustment

Tai Chi movement is not only for quiet people who are looking for a form of gentle exercise. It is also the best means of adjustment available for people who are very active physically and who want to key themselves down to a state of normal functioning. When a person is extremely overtired or tries to stop suddenly after engaging in very strenuous physical exertion, he may find that he is unable to rest. If a person forces oneself to rest in such a condition, physical damage will be caused. The same holds true when one is going from a state of deep meditation or relaxation to a state of normal activity. It is also very different to adjust.

Harmony with Nature

Tai Chi movement integrates all aspects of one's being and brings one into harmony with the natural law of the universe. Through the practice of Tai Chi movement, one can learn to recognize and correct habits which violate the principles of the universe and cause ill health and disharmony. If one is unaware of the natural laws of the universe, it is easy to violate them and as a result, there is always a loss of balance and harmony, both internally and externally[1]. If these imbalances persist, they destroy physical and mental health.

When an individual's energy system is in a state of disorder and imbalance, the corresponding energies mirrored in the macrocosm reflect this disorder and lack of harmony. By balancing one's own internal energies and applying the natural laws discovered through Tai Chi movement practice in daily life, a harmonious response from the universe naturally results. When every facet of one's life is an expression of natural law, one is spontaneously in tune with the universe.

Immune System Enhancement

I (OmNi) recently read a report from mainland China in which two groups of people took a test. The first group of 15 older people were from age 58 to 65. The second group of 25 younger people were from age 18 to 25. Every morning, the older group went to a park to do Tai Chi movement, while the younger group walked twenty minutes from their homes to a park to go running. The older people were at a general level in Tai Chi movement, and some of them may have had illnesses or physical difficulties. They followed the instruction and walked to the park, which was good exercise, and then the instructor taught Tai Chi movement for 15 minutes. They practiced a set of 24 movements, which were a simplified form of Tai Chi movement. Meanwhile, the younger group ran one thousand six hundred meters (one mile).

One day, the researchers had both groups take some saliva from their mouths before and after their exercise to test the body's reaction to the different kinds of exercise. In the Tai Chi group, the researchers discovered that two-thirds of the people showed an increase in a kind of immune protein called SIGA. That immune protein helps people be healthy, strong, and look young. Thus the older people, after walking and practicing 15 minutes of Tai Chi movement, increased their immune power. For the young ones who ran, the saliva test showed that the immune protein, SIGA, decreased.

When you do Tai Chi practice, you should keep the tip of your tongue touching the upper palate. This connects the internal channels of the body and enhances the internal circulation of energy (see Chapter 8). If the joggers had touched their tongues to their palates and given up drinking soft drinks, you might expect the results to be the same as those of the Tai Chi practitioners. But the speed and mechanical repitition of jogging cannot produce the same results as gentle movement. Jogging is a fiery sport.

The internal practice of holding the tongue up is not only for exercise but is good to do in general circumstances as well. A bridge is formed by holding up the tongue. Talking or drinking too much breaks that energy connection.

Body-Mind Integration

Through the consistent practice of Tai Chi gentle exercise, one may strengthen and integrate one's physical and mental functions. Generally, people either engage in mental activity and are oblivious to their bodies, or they engage in physical activity but their minds are wandering and not aware of what the body is doing. In this way, they create a split between body and mind, which are essentially one inseparable system.

Consciousness directly influences the energy flow and the general state of energy. The fact that this split is created and that body and mind do not function as one unit greatly impairs the ability to realize one's full potential. Nerve synapses atrophy from lack of use and vast areas of the brain lie dormant. Input from the external environment is inaccurately or incompletely transmitted to the brain, which in turn relays faulty messages as a response. As a result of this, the nervous system never fully develops and the awareness of reality, both internal and external, is vastly distorted.

At first, some people find Tai Chi movements difficult to imitate, because they are unable to combine the internal with the external – which means they cannot combine the subtle energy of their minds and spirits with the grosser physical energy of their bodies. The purpose of Tai Chi gentle exercise is not merely to achieve a certain standard of external movement and physical control, as in sports and dance. In order to perform Tai Chi movement, the main requirement is that when the body moves, the qi and spirit also move.

This is achieved in the following manner: before starting to move, one empties the mind of all extraneous thought. Only when the mind is calm and unoccupied is one able to focus and direct it at will. When the movements are performed, they are done so very slowly. This allows the mind to pay attention to every detail of the body's movement. Physical strength is never employed to move the body. One combines the power of one's breath and subtle energy to propel the body. When the mind follows every detail of the body's activity, it affects the state of one's physical energy. The energy transforms from a distinct, individualized state to an undifferentiated, vaporized and electrical state.

The changing of physical energy to the vaporized and electrical states is a natural phenomenon in the body. The use of this specific type of movement creates the integration of energy. Not only do one's internal energies become integrated, but the internal energies also integrate with the energy of the environment in which one is practicing the movement. When one's energy is harmonized through movement, it is no longer merely physical energy, but is combined with the energy of the mind and spirit as one integral whole. This is why it is said that Tai Chi movement reunites all aspect of one's being in undivided oneness.

Personality Development

No possession in the world is more valuable than a stable, pleasant personality. Despite the fact that there are many different techniques which attempt to improve the personality, it is rarely realized that personality is in essence an expression of the energy embodied by an individual. Modern psychological techniques may attempt to work on the mind through such means as positive thinking or various methods of mind control. Yet any technique which addresses itself only to the mind is dealing with form while ignoring substance.

For example, when "positive thinking" is stressed, two problems may be encountered. Positive thinking may keep a person in the realm of make-believe, preventing him or her from facing the reality of life; and excessive positivity which denies the potentiality of the opposite polarity may lead a person into difficulty by encouraging mental rigidity. The key to cultivating a balanced personality is to harmonize one's yin and yang elements. Since a person's personality is the expression of his energy, it follows that if a person's energy is rough, unrefined and unbalanced, his personality will express the same qualities. The way to improve the personality, then, is to transform the quality of one's energy, to refine the coarseness and equalize the imbalances.

By learning Tai Chi movement, a person can effectively overcome all shortcomings of personality which are due to incompleteness and imbalance of energy. Tai Chi movement accomplishes this without the need for any dogma or belief to control or restrain people. It improves the personality by refining and harmonizing the person's yin and yang energies, resulting in an even temperament and calm disposition. These qualities enable one to remain poised even through the most difficult situations. To be excessively negative is a form of madness, yet to be excessively positive is equally a form of madness. The way to avoid the duality of mind is through integrating all mental elements and functions. When the state of mental harmony is achieved, one's whole being is in consonance of its own accord.

Gentle Physical Movement Enlivens You

When you dance, sing a song or listen to a funny joke, you feel enlivened or younger. Dancing, singing or painting naturally affect your emotions and indirectly aid your internal system.

However, the practice of gentle physical movement like Tai Chi does even more to enliven and invigorate you than the arts. It works directly on your internal harmonization and adjustment. This is why, as you become more balanced, you also feel great pleasure. Gentle movement like tai chi and qigong has a self-generating, rejuvenating, lubricating (by stimulating all types of internal secretions) and refreshing effect.

If you consistently practice gentle movement, you will refresh yourself internally all the time. Whether you do it each morning or evening, or both morning and evening, and whether you do the whole set, half of the set, or even repeat just one movement, it is all beneficial.

A baby's entire body is light, soft and supple. Each muscle, tendon and bone has the resilience of the tender new life within. Gentle movement refreshes you so that your body feels like a baby's[2].

People who do this exercise may seem to age just like everybody else, but they are internally different. They are refreshed clear down to the marrow of their bones, which actually slows down the aging process.

Self-Control

Self-control is an important result of practicing gentle physical movement like Tai Chi and one that enables you to avoid creating new predicaments for yourself. Instead of fighting and trying to control others, you are able to control yourself more skillfully. Even fighting is the art of skillfully controlling your own movement.

The true triumph in life is self-control, not the conquest of someone else. Sun Tzu, a Taoist strategist who wrote the classic *The Art of War*, said, "The high art of war is not waging battle, but making peace." Without fighting, you can still overcome trouble; better yet, you will be able to avoid problems in your life. Fighting usually causes even more trouble than you had in the first place.

Once you have learned self-control, and once you can skillfully control your own movements, you can arrange things in your environment so that you are undefeatable or invincible. You cannot be defeated because you can defend yourself well and your self-control is so good. By not defeating others, they win and you win also.

Physical movement is a spiritual practice that brings about self-development and virtue. Harmony is the virtue that results from self-control and appropriate action in all situations. This approach dissolves the sense of life as a battle and helps you rise above the pressures of the lower sphere of life. You learn to go beyond confrontation, contention, the network of worldly life and the engagement of emotion. You learn to go beyond a bad choice in a relationship, natural obligation, physical obligation and so forth. True development is not found in dramatic public performances but in everyday life.

Tai Chi movement is an intense training of both body and mind which enables them to function as one unit rather than separately. When defending oneself in martial arts, for example, one small mistake either in skill, temperament or disposition will cause one to be the loser. Tai Chi movement trains a person to be calm, to have self-control, and to integrate these qualities with the internal techniques of fighting. The ability to achieve this integration can greatly benefit anyone who practices Kung Fu, boxing, Karate, or any other martial art. Through Tai Chi movement, a professional fighter may learn more about control and balance in fighting. And even if a person who practices Tai Chi movement has had no special training in self-defense, if the occasion should arise in which he needs to protect himself, he will spontaneously be prepared to do so. Tai Chi movement practiced as a martial art relies on the projection of qi toward one's opponent rather than on fighting technique. Strengthening oneself for fighting is not the direction of the Integral Way[3]. The strength of health is of correct value to all generations.

Personal Enjoyment

For later practitioners of physical art, especially my (OmNi's) generation, the definition of the internal school has changed. Qi movement is not only for gaining internal strength, but also for pure personal pleasure. Our experience and purpose in practicing Tai Chi movement is not to compete against someone else or to guard ourselves physically. We do it for pure pleasure. We are already confident that we can cope with situations, and we are already healthy. The four types of standing movement that we practice are the simple pleasure of our lives. Sometimes we do it gently, and sometimes we do it vigorously, but never like the external school.

Some people take pleasure in watching movies, eating tasty food, reading an interesting book, meeting a good friend or doing other nice things. Practitioners of Tai Chi can do those things too, but they have one more pleasure in addition to that: chi movement. Most people do not know about it, and that is why we teach it. The external school does it for show or fighting, but never just for fun.

When you learn the Way, you come to know that the Way is in everyone and everything. Applying the Way in your life makes your life fuller, more interesting and more enjoyable. The Way leads to good, productive fun, not the destructive kind of excitement that comes from drugs or alcohol. The pure pleasure and joy that come from your practice are more practical and lasting than other types of fun.

The secret to following the Way or learning qi movement is to enjoy yourself. The principle of Lao Tzu is "wu wei" which, practically speaking, means that if you are not too serious about spiritual achievement, you will achieve yourself naturally, just by continuing to practice.

Tai Chi and the Healing Professions

People who practice boxing, weight lifting, gymnastics and sports produce energy, but it is not healing energy. Healing energy is much deeper than muscular energy. Almost all medical professions, not only acupuncturists but also surgeons, dentists, etc., require dexterity. Sports affect how you manage yourself and can make you unable to fulfill certain skills gracefully or suitably. This is why learning Tai Chi or Chi Kung is recommended for all types of healing professions. For people with spiritual interest and a delicate profession, practicing any of these arts is a cultivation that will assist your development and probably bring about the breakthrough you have been working on for many years.

Tai Chi and Longevity

Tai Chi can be of interest for young people who would like to develop their potential in life. For people of middle age and older, Tai Chi is a way to improve their health.

When we focus on the subjects of physical health and longevity, it is important to remember that all life needs movement. The entire universe is constantly moving in all types of circles, big and small, horizontal and vertical. Any linear movement always comes to an end, but transforming a straight line into a circle makes it never-ending. Tai Chi movement is a non-stop movement; you become inexhaustible when you do it. You never run out of energy or become worn out.

The ancient developed ones discovered that cyclic movement is the basis of the universe, with all the heavenly bodies always moving in their own orbits. That kind of discovery was inspiring to ancient people. It is one example of the way in which they learned from nature. One of the first things they learned from nature was to not cease moving.

In some cultures, people think that it is noble to be idle and have someone else, such as a servant, do everything for them, but that goes against the nature of life. We should value all opportunities to move, because natural movement promotes health and longevity.

During the Ching Dynasty, Tai Chi became famous among the practitioners of all types of martial arts, because its approach was not that of brute force. However, those who turn Tai Chi into a fighting tool pay the high price of shortening their lives. That is not the fault of the exercise itself, but the tension that martial arts champions create around it. It is not normal or natural to live with that kind of tension, day and night thinking about a possible surprise attack. Although such a practitioner may learn to relax physically, mentally they are still tense. The result is that they are soon killed, not by their opponent but by excessive tension.

Lao Tzu, Chuang Tzu and many others practiced qi exercise. However, tai chi was the principle of their whole life, not just a form of exercise. Tai Chi or Qigong movements were merely reflections of this deep principle of life.

For many years I (OmNi) have observed those who do movements like Tai Chi Exercise or Qigong and those who do not do them. For those who do them, the minimum attainment is to look 5 to 10 years younger than those who do not. The median attainment is to look 10 to 20 years younger, and the maximum attainment is to look 30 to 40 years younger. It is possible to attain still higher. Each individual needs to adjust or attune oneself to make the best of such a profound practice.

Some famous people who achieved physical longevity were the Yellow Emperor, Niao, Shun and Yu, all of whom lived over 100 years. It is said that Pong Tzu lived to be over 800 years old, and Lao Tzu lived 160 or 200 years according to Ssu Ma Chien, a reliable historian of the Han Dynasty. There was also

Li Pa Ba and many others in the ancient tradition. A couple of Zahn (Zen or Chan) Masters also enjoyed a lifetime of 120 years.

Today, many people worry not just about the length of their life, but about their ability to be healthy and happy when they are older. Qi exercise not only prolongs life, it improves your physical energy foundation for a more vigorous, healthy and happy life at any age. Self-cultivators appreciate the value of an enduring and untiring spirit that can live in a disturbing world.

Gentle Qigong or Tai Chi is not like cardio-vascular aerobic exercises that are popular in technologically advanced societies. People in China, who regularly practice gentle movement, live to be 80 or 90 without ever developing heart disease or high blood pressure or other age related diseases that are common in the United States. Millions of Chinese people go out every morning at 5 a.m. to do qi exercises. Some of them are quite advanced in age, yet they still have vitality and exuberance because their qi is strong. Everyone has the potential to master their own body and their own qi by cultivating themselves and thus preventing the decline in health that happens to so many older people.

Tai Chi and Spiritual Growth

In addition to improving your health, Tai Chi also guides you to refine your personal energy from coarse to fine to exquisite. When I (OmNi) was young, I had a special opportunity to learn gentle physical arts from my father's teachers and friends, who were very special people.

We have a great devotion to these movements, because they are a practical way to learn about one's spirit. If you pay close attention to what you are doing, you can learn something about spiritual truth by learning about its opposite, the physical realm.

Some monks take pride in being able to recite a few holy scriptures, thinking this can help their souls. However, a spiritually achieved person understands that continually repeating anything will deplete one's vitality and be of no benefit. A wise student will practice physical arts like Tai Chi to attain a balanced view of life and a well-developed soul that is impartial and complete. The physical arts are actually a type of prayer for harmonization with universal nature.

Art is different from science. A scientific conclusion is not anyone's personal truth, but is a common standard. Art, on the other hand, is personal or individual. It can be common truth also, but it allows unlimited personal achievement. The learning of the Way is artistic, but it is also scientific. It is the process of discovering the common truth by dissolving the personal self, which is usually an accumulation of incomplete and distorted impressions from human life and culture.

To dissolve the self and restore our natural life, we learn practices from the healthy artistic sphere of life. When you become totally united with the movement, you dissolve your internal cultural distortions and are able to experience your original self. Each movement comes from the deep universal nature, which finds its expression through you. This art of life is, at the same time, the art of mind, the art of spirit, and the wordless expression of cosmic or universal law.

People usually enjoy sensory excitement or experiences of success. Tai Chi is a different enjoyment because it is spiritual enjoyment. Although it takes practice, once you achieve it you have a tremendous joy that cannot be compared to anything else. You find completeness inside and out. You find your "self" in each movement, yet it is no longer a narrow sense of self, because you join with the universe. Spiritual development does not happen by talking or by writing books; it occurs when you reach the same vibrational frequency as deep nature.

The most important element in life is the spirit. When you do gentle movement, you are not doing the exercise alone; all the spirits of your life are enjoying themselves[4]. This is called "uniting with the great universe." During your exercise, there is no more separation, no more obstruction between the external and internal worlds. You feel the air around you, because your practice develops a special spiritual sensitivity. You feel the energy field outside and the energy field inside merge and integrate.

From movement, you discover the truth that the movement embodies cosmic law. You experience the universe revolving and evolving. You become a heavenly body, and you and the universe together become one united heavenly body. You unite with Heaven by always moving in cyclic patterns. All of nature moves with you, never getting stuck in any single spot. This is a high enjoyment in human spiritual life.

Scarecrows in the fields are stuffed with straw. However, wise people do not like to be stuffed with straw. They replace the "junk" that occupies too much of their time and consumes too much of their energy with ancient arts and skills that fill them with the high vitality of spiritual essence instead of consuming them.

5 Brief History of Tai Chi Chuan

Internal and External Schools of Physical Arts

The physical arts that are part of Chinese culture are of two schools: external and internal. The external school teaches regular martial arts that increase one's fighting skill and strength. Everything is on the external level of performance.

The internal school developed from external martial arts and may be used for self-defense in an emergency, but its main purpose is health and physical education and the refinement of individual physical energy. In other words, it can be described as a physical art for a spiritual purpose. What it teaches is not for display to others, but to strengthen oneself internally.

This is the basic difference between the external and internal schools. However, this classification is not absolute. Even people who learn to use or increase their external strength often find that they need a good, strong internal foundation, thus the external school also has internal practices. Yet the direction of the two schools is essentially different.

The external school, especially Shao Lin is very popular in China, as is karate in Japan, tae kwon do in Korea, although the common source of all these practices is China. The internal school is appreciated by gentle people and a somewhat smaller number of extremely dedicated students who learn spiritual development from achieved teachers.

Typically, for any physical movement to survive and be promoted to young people in Chinese society, it must be a martial art. Young people want to learn something that can provide protection, so they are attracted to quick attack and forceful movements. Internal practice is totally different. No force can be seen when energy moves internally.

The internal school, which originated from martial arts, evolved beyond external moves when highly achieved martial arts practitioners realized that true protection comes from good health and good energy and from having the wisdom to apply that energy correctly in the world. Lasting protection does not come from quick, forceful movements.

In northern China, some practitioners of Ba Gua[1] are very forceful and can defend themselves or attack others if they wish. This is the fundamental motive underlying their practice. The internal school, on the other hand, is like a walking stick that you automatically know how to use if you need to. Physical movement lays down the principle, but the learning is spiritual. This focus produces an entirely different result than martial arts, namely evenness, balance, smoothness, kindness, openness, harmlessness and generosity. These virtues can guide your life to high and beautiful fulfillment rather than toward the destructive skill of killing.

Bruce Lee, a young practitioner of Chinese martial arts, introduced these arts to the West and made them popular. Seeing this, the Chinese renewed their own interest in the old physical arts.

Self-defense is instinctual in all animals and it is a side effect of the internal school. The benefit of these arts is like that of a walking stick when climbing a steep mountain. You can make your climb easier, and if the end of the stick has a hook on it, then you can use it to support you at the right time.

In ancient times, external schools had a simple requirement for achievement: if you had strong muscles, you were a good fighter and a winner of competitions. Physical strength can certainly do many things, but if you want to learn how to expand your energy and apply it, or if you want to experience a different sphere of life that is intangible and everlasting, internal qi movement is perhaps the best way to achieve these goals.

The internal school redirected the purpose of martial arts toward the internal practice of energy circulation. Circulating energy internally makes a person strong, thus one side effect of internal practice is to actually be a better martial artist.

There is another difference between martial arts and gentle movement. Martial arts psychologically prepare you to fight, but in gentle Tai Chi movement, there is no rival other than yourself. When you bring yourself together in one piece using these highly developed physical arts, you achieve balance, poise and self-confidence and become non-aggressive.

We consider traditional Tai Chi or Qigong practices as physical arts instead of martial arts. Martial arts are less important in modern times, while internal physical arts are always beneficial.

We would say that modern students should not be so insistent about their school being better than others. Some schools promote the martial arts, but martial arts are very limited. Each student should also learn the principles of movement from the *I Ching*[2], and the principle of balance between yin and yang from the *Tao Te Ching*. Those books are the source of Tai Chi movement.

Master Zhang San-Feng

A clear record of the history of Tai Chi Chuan was kept by Mr. Wang Chun-Shi, a great scholar who lived at the end of the Ming Dynasty. His son Wang Pa-Chia wrote down Chen Chow-Tung's description of this art and passed it down to Chang Shoong-Chee and from him to Wang Cheng-Nang.

Much later than Kou Hong, Master Zhang San-Feng who lived during the Sung Dynasty (960-1279 C.E.) pursued the Way and achieved himself. He began to use the name "the internal school" to describe his type of martial art.

Later, another Master Zhang San-Feng lived during part of the Yuan Dynasty (1200-1367 C.E.) and the Ming Dynasty (1368-1643 C.E.). He further developed the art of the internal school. Because they have the same spirit, the internal school and the school of swordsmanship are actually the same school with different names. The internal school is the more popular of the two.

Many students thought that these two masters, both named Zhang San-Feng, were the same person because the names were the same. However, the first Master Zhang San-Feng was described as having started the art of the internal school by spiritual inspiration while carrying out his duty of protecting a delivery of herbs to the Emperor. While traveling to the capital, Master Zhang San-Feng and the carriers spent the night at a roadside temple. A spirit, the main god of the temple, Shuan Ti (the authority of the North Star), taught Master Zhang San-Feng the art of using the sword in a dream. The next day, he and his carriers were besieged by a group of bandits who wished to take the herbs. With a single sword, Master Zhang San-Feng defeated over a hundred bandits. In this way, without having learned external martial arts, he came to be respected as the initiating master of the internal school.

The later Master Zhang San-Feng is much more renowned for his immortal achievement, but there is no direct record of his being involved with the arts. Even so, it passed from teacher to students and he was believed to have started Tai Chi Chuan. He may have further developed the art of the internal school begun by the former Master Zhang San-Feng.

It is possible that the two Masters Zhang San-Feng were actually only one person. It is also possible that they were two and the second continued the work of the former, but the truth is not known and is only a matter of speculation. It is not uncommon for a spiritual life to be like uncontrolled dragon energy. We accept what the teachers of the last generation taught without making any personal assertion.

The question of whether Tai Chi Chuan was the art of the first Master Zhang San-Feng has never been answered. There are minor differences in the names of the movements. The focus on single movement practice was emphasized more than the practice of the whole series of movements that we now have.

There is another anecdote about Master Zhang San-Feng. It was told that one day, he was meditating in Wu Dang Shan, where he lived after accomplishing the special errand of carrying herbs to the Emperor. There he saw a crane and a snake fighting and was inspired by them. The snake, by following the naturally smooth, winding and swift movements of its body, can usually escape the sharp beak of the crane. However, the crane has a long neck which is similar to the body of a snake. A crane can be trained, or learn from the snake, how to develop a similar movement; then the crane will not lose the battle. In other words, a crane needs to develop its skill. This confirms an important principle in physical art, which is practice.

Master Zhang San-Feng found this fight interesting and inspiring. He integrated what he learned from the snake and the crane into his practice and was believed to have developed the art of Ba Gua movement and further developed the art of the internal school.

The Chen Family

Another account of the origin of Tai Chi movement is that the first Tai Chi movement was passed down from Master Zhang San-Feng to Wang Tzung, who passed it to two students. One student was Chen Chow-Tung of Wenchow, and the other person was Jiang Fa of Hunan. Jiang Fa's teaching seems to have disappeared.

The popular Chen family of Hunan, famous for Tai Chi Chuan, declared that their Tai Chi was developed by their own ancestors and that they had not learned from Jiang Fa. Although in reality their statement may be inaccurate, the descendants of the Chen family were truthful, because they were born much later and they could not verify what they thought they knew.

However, practitioners in a nearby town passed down a different story about the Chen family. They said that the Chen family of Hunan had learned from Jiang Fa and had spread the art of internal Tai Chi Chuan to neighboring regions.

Master Chen Tuan and Tai Chi

The *I Ching* and the *Tao Te Ching* are two important teachings in the ancient teaching of the Integral Way. During the end of the Tang Dynasty, a great sage was born. That was the time when society was confused. He did not earn a position as ruler or adviser to a ruler, but he contributed to the peace of China during that period of history by guiding young people to achieve it. He was Master Chen Tuan[3]. Also, by his profound study of the *I Ching*, he refreshed the vision of all the Confucian scholars and brought about the reintegration of Taoism and Confucianism.

The practice of Tai Chi Chuan was started by Master Zhang San-Feng, a realizer of the natural spiritual truth who received the influence of Master Chen Tuan, but with good spiritual development. He lived in Wu Dang Mountain where Master Chen Tuan lived in his early stage of his spiritual cultivation. The Tai Chi principle as ancient cosmology of integral spiritual vision can be credited to Master Chen Tuan. Around 100 years later, according to existing records, Master Zhang was inspired in a vision brought to him by a spiritual authority, a god of mystical Heaven, Shuan Ti. Master Zhang San-Feng or some other achieved one initiated the combination of quietude in movement. He integrated both, so that where there is movement, there is stillness, and where there is calmness, there is activity.

Therefore, Tai Chi Chuan is not just another program from somebody's intellectual mind; although it is told that it is the inspiration of spirits, we think it is a fruit of nature. It deeply integrates the principles of the *I Ching*.

Modern Schools of Tai Chi

From Zhang San-Feng, Tai Chi was transmitted down through the generations and many traditions and styles developed. Today, the Yang, Chen, Wu, Hao, and Sun styles are most commonly encountered and there are numerous books, magazine articles, and internet websites devoted to them. However, there are other lesser known (esoteric) styles of Tai Chi such as Cheng Man Ching Style Tai Chi, Taiji 13 Gestures, Wu Dang Style Tai Chi, Li Style Tai Chi, Chang Style Tai Chi and four styles of our Taoist family tradition (Harmony Tai Chi, Gentle Path Tai Chi, Sky Journey Tai Chi, and Infinite Expansion Tai Chi).

PART TWO:
TAI CHI PRINCIPLES

6 The Tai Chi Principle

The integration of yin and yang is called Tai Chi.

Everything that exists is an expression of Tai Chi.

Every small particle is a Tai Chi.

The vast universe is a Tai Chi.

The gathering of small events or units is a Tai Chi.

The dispersion of the vast universe is a Tai Chi.

There is nothing beyond Tai Chi or excluded from it.

Thus, the individual body is a Tai Chi.

The cosmic body is also a Tai Chi.

Tai Chi is the integral truth of the Universe.

(from the *Hua Hu Ching*)[1]

The basic principle of the teaching of the Way is the principle of tai chi. Tai Chi as a principle is somewhat different from Tai Chi movement. Tai Chi movement demonstrates the cosmic principle of tai chi. When we practice Tai Chi movement we benefit from the tai chi principle and can apply our learning in our daily contact with everyone and everything.

The principle or philosophy of tai chi started simply. Approximately ten thousand years ago, people's consciousness started to grow. Although it was not fully developed intellectually, there was an awareness of the difference between night and day, male and female, etc. As people continued to develop, they discovered that everything has two opposing sides, which they called yin and yang. On a mountain, one side faces south and the other faces north, and the vegetation is different on each side. In this way, a mountain also has a yin and a yang.

Humans have a top and bottom. The top is yang and the bottom is yin. You also have a right side and a left side. The left side is yang and the right side is yin. Similarly, the front is yin and the back is yang.

Tai chi is the principle of unity; yin and yang are its manifestations. Without yin and yang, the unity cannot be seen. If you are aware of this principle, you will notice that whenever a person starts to move or do something, their movement creates a discrimination between yin and yang. For example, when we are walking, our left and right legs alternate to keep us moving. That is the basic interpretation of tai chi. Both sides, help each other. If a thing stays still and does not reach the conscious level, there is unity or integralness, and you do not differentiate its parts.

In personal relationships of any kind, there is always an interplay of yin and yang. If harmony is produced, then it is a positive situation. If one side overextends itself, then imbalance, disharmony or destruction will be seen. To manage our lives well, we need to achieve tai chi or balance. Imbalance and disharmony go against the principle of tai chi, and anything that goes against the principle of tai chi will fail, decline and end, unless balance and harmony are restored.

The unity and harmony of tai chi are expressed when: 1) your mind does not fight your spirit, 2) your spirit does not fight your mind, 3) your body does not fight your mind, 4) your physical desire does not fight your mind.

An individual person is a small model of tai chi, internally and externally. When there is disharmony, you lose your balance and disturb the natural balance of tai chi. It is important to be aware when that happens.

In Tai Chi practice, always watch how your energy is flowing. Is it flowing well or not? If one part of the body or one movement is overextended, it creates a blockage in your energy flow. Blockage indicates imbalance, and you must correct yourself to follow the principle of tai chi.

Conceptual and ideological conflicts are common in today's world, but they are superficial and reflect nothing other than narrow-mindedness. The human basics are: "I am a tai chi, and the world is a tai chi. Are things in order between me and society?" If there is harmony and balance, tai chi is there; you will be happy with your environment, and your environment will be happy too. When anything differs from this, there is difficulty and something needs to be corrected.

The most important thing in your Tai Chi practice is to observe that when your outside moves, is the inside moving too? If the inside is not moving, then you are not united. Even without unifying themselves inside, ambitious leaders say, "I am going to unify the whole world!" That is a fantasy. It cannot be that way.

The Way, The Tai Chi Principle, and Tai Chi Movement

What we teach is not folk or religious Taoism, but the true spiritual achievement of the ancients. Harmony and balance are the basic principles of life. Beyond that, what else can be said? Not much. The most important thing is whether we can achieve normalcy in our lives. Are our minds aligned with the tai chi principle at each moment? What besides this can be called the Way?

The Way (Tao) is not something outside of us that we can pursue or worship. We need to realize the tai chi principle of harmony and balance in our daily lives. The Way is not a conceptual activity. It is life itself, in its totality. We are all the offspring of nature, and each of us is a small model of nature. To be the Way is more important than talking about what the Way is.

We are naturally born as a tai chi, but after experiencing worldly life, we are affected by our surroundings. We need to examine how well we handle the effects of life around us. If we become upset when we cannot achieve something or if we are bothered by someone who has a bad attitude toward us or who does not play fair, how are we to respond? In Tai Chi movement, we learn not to fight but to yield. If people attack you, a gentle movement can transform the situation. A tai chi can always move around. If you allow yourself to move, the attack remains only a situation and does not escalate into something more.

On the other hand, it may not be someone else who is bothering you. Maybe the real problem is that you are not conscious enough and are therefore bothering someone else. In that case, you need to immediately correct yourself. In any situation, we must move just right; not too much, not too little. If we move too little, friction or conflict comes. If we move too much, we exhaust ourselves and are trapped.

We cannot leave the world to seek peace. There is no peace in life. There is no total security. If you think you need security, stand right here where you are and do Tai Chi movement. It will protect you and not damage anyone else. We believe all of you are wise enough to move without creating problems, but sometimes you need to watch your emotions, especially toward yourself. You say, "Damn this, damn that," and become really unhappy. Allow yourself to move around with Tai Chi movement. If you move too far in one direction, you have nowhere to go and have to turn around. This is important to remember.

Some of you may think that a spiritual life consists of meditating all day long. That is not the Way; that is a dead end. The real practitioner of the Way keeps moving. We enjoy our lives and enjoy tai chi. Tai Chi is accomplished through our lives. Each moment is a self-accomplishing completeness.

You might ask us, "How can you describe movement without talking about stillness?" Do you really think that there is no movement in stillness? Even when you do not move, you are still moving, but the movement is subtle. You are breathing and thinking; strongly or gently, you are doing something. If you do not keep moving, your body will deteriorate. Life itself is movement.

Our destiny in each moment is to move correctly and sustain the natural flow of life within us. Maybe you think you need to surpass your destiny by going to a mountain where you can stop moving and breathing and fossilize yourself, but is that really surpassing life? Life and nature are constantly living, moving, working and generating. Once we stop generating, we degenerate.

Each cell of your body is a tai chi. We are each a small model of the universe, thus we are each a small but complete tai chi. Inside, we are composed of even smaller tai chi's that need us to keep moving. An even temper, pleasant nature, healthful life, youthful appearance, and everything fine about you, all come from good movement. The Way includes both movement and stillness. It is from stillness that we learn to move. Many years ago, we were stones.

7 Tai Chi Movement, Universal Law, and the Law of Individual Being

Ancient achieved people deeply observed the operation of nature and developed a series of movements based on cosmology and patterned after the movement of the universe. Tai Chi movement is one of the most popular of these systems. Based on the principle that the human body is a miniature universe, the system of gentle movement aims to guide an individual's energy through his or her microcosmic energy network (see Chapter 8) in a manner which exactly follows cosmic law. By consistently harmonizing oneself with cosmic law in this way, physical health improves, the mind becomes clear, and the spirit becomes strong and tranquil.

It is the virtue or inherent quality of the universe to support all life. However, violation of universal law cuts one off from that support. Tai Chi movement provides the means by which realignment with universal law may occur. In this way, one may enjoy the support of the universe in all aspects of life. Through the practice of Tai Chi movement, the intellectual concept of the laws of nature is transformed into actual physical experience. By observing how one's own body and energy operate while performing Tai Chi movement, one may discover experientially the law inherent in individual being. When one knows the law of individual being one knows the law of the universe.

The exploration of Tao as universal law through the practice of Tai Chi movement begins with an understanding of the concepts of Taoist cosmology. However, it is only through experiencing the validity of universal law that its power to transform one's life can be realized.

Undivided Oneness (Wu Chi) – The Root of All Movement

The first principle of Tai Chi movement is that undivided oneness is the root of all movement. From the perspective of cosmology, undivided oneness is the origin of every manifestation in the universe. As the undivided oneness of the primal energy (wu chi) moves, it polarizes, creating yin and yang. The interactions and combinations of the polarities resulting from this movement bring forth the myriad manifestations. Thus undivided oneness is the source of both the evolution and devolution of the multi-universe.

> The universal subtle essence gave birth to the One.
> One gave birth to Two.
> Two gave birth to Three.
> Three gave birth to the Myriad Things.
> (Lao Tzu, from *The Tao Te Ching*)[1]

Tai Chi is the integration of yin and yang polarities. The polarization of the primal energy as it alternates between yin and yang is not a divisive or separating process. The polarizing movement is always integrated by the power of undivided oneness. If it were a division rather than an integrated movement, the multi-universe would inevitably come to an end. An illustration of undivided oneness might be the way a person uses each leg alternately in the process of walking. Each leg cooperates with the other and both are governed by the oneness of the person who is walking. The principle of undivided oneness applies in Tai Chi movement as well as in the reality of daily life.

When we are born, our body, mind and spirit are perfectly harmonized and integrated. However, in the process of living in the world, the body, mind and spirit drift farther and farther apart until their ultimate disintegration, which is death. At death, the soul or yang polarity returns to the subtle realm and the body or yin polarity to the physical realm. A human being dies because he is no longer able to integrate the yin and yang vibrational polarities of his being. The shen, the energy responsible for the organization of the individual being, no longer functions to integrate and direct its energies, and the po (yin) and the hun (yang), the I (yin) and the chih (yang), cannot fulfill their respective functions[2].

The multi-universe is infinite because it continuously integrates its polarities through its exquisite pattern of movement. In the human body, Tai Chi movement brings physical, emotional, mental and spiritual energies into alignment once again as undivided oneness (wu chi). When a person achieves the integration of his own internal polarities through the practice of Tai Chi movement, this in turn will cause the response of harmony and unification of all the apparent opposites which appear externally and internally in his life.

The term used to describe the undivided oneness, the source of all movement, is wu chi, the Infinite One or the Ultimate Oneness. You may say that tai chi, the natural law, proceeds from wu chi. Yet wu chi is in tai chi and tai chi is contained in wu chi. There is no separation between the conditions of Tai Chi and wu chi, just as there is no separation between yin and yang and undivided oneness.

Yin and Yang and the Principle of Symmetry

All movement may be explained in terms of yin and yang. For example, leftward movement is yang, rightward movement is yin. Upward movement is yang, downward movement is yin. Exhalation is yang, inhalation is yin, and so forth. The movements of Tai Chi exercise are a continual sequence of yin and yang movements. If there is an upward movement, then there is a low movement to balance it. If there is a movement to the left, then there is a movement to the right to give it symmetry. Inhalation and exhalation are also coordinated with each movement so that yin and yang, which are sometimes also called the negative and positive vibrational polarities of the human energy system, are always balanced.

The Alternation of Stillness and Movement

Through their deep observation of the movement and development of the universe, the ancient developed people discovered the natural law that stillness and movement alternately follow each other. In the general sense, movement is yang and stillness is yin. Many spiritual traditions emphasize quiet sitting meditation. Yet quiet sitting alone tends to wither one's vitality because it causes one's energy to stagnate. If one practices quiet sitting exclusively, one hastens the degeneration of one's life, rather than furthering one's spiritual evolution.

In the Integral Way, it is understood that in order to derive full benefit from quiet sitting meditation, it must be balanced by activity. Tai Chi movement is a moving meditation which provides the perfect balance to quiet sitting. Each activity enhances the other to move one forward toward complete spiritualization. When active, look for stillness in the activity. When engaged in quiet sitting meditation, find the creative animation in the stillness. In all things, combine and integrate all apparent opposites as undivided oneness.

Gentle Rhythmic Versus Hasty Violent Movements

Another universal principle revealed in Tai Chi movement is the principle that sudden movement causes energy to stagnate, while gentle, rhythmic movement brings about its flow. Sudden movement must always stop quickly. Inevitably there is a pause or the inhibition of the energy flow. Similar to this is the principle that hasty action ultimately results in slowness because it quickly exhausts one's energy, while gentle rhythmic movement can be continued with great endurance. With this logic, we can understand that those who are violent can afford only one show of force at a time, and are weak in reality. Yet those who move in a gentle rhythm can keep going continually and prove to be the strongest. As another example, if a person decides to go to a distant place and tries to run all the way, he becomes exhausted before reaching his destination. But if he walks at a comfortable pace, he will eventually get there. This is a fundamental principle of Tai Chi movement and indicates the "constant virtue" or constant quality inherent in gentle rhythmic movement.

The Circularity of All Natural Movement

The natural movement of everything in the universe follows a circular pattern. The earth spins on its axis as it orbits the sun. The sun, in turn, orbits the galactic center of the Milky Way. The Milky Way follows a circular pattern as it courses through the universe. Life itself consists of cycles and the energies of the human organism also circulate through their microcosmic energy network. All of the movements of Tai Chi are a series of circles which reflect this eternal, cosmic law.

The Law of Reversion: Returning to the Source

Everything in nature follows a cyclical process of growth and evolution. All things grow and develop and, after their peak has been reached, revert back to their source to regenerate again and again. The movement of evolution is not a linear process. Anything which continues in a straight line must eventually run out of power and come to an end. The multi-universe is able to continue its process of evolution eternally because it reverts to its source for regeneration before reaching the absolute end of its impetus. You may say that the energy is recycled.

This is an essential principle of Tai Chi movement. In movement, one never extends one's body or energy completely because this will leave one with no energy in reserve. Instead, one goes only to a certain point, and then draws inward again to the center to gather one's energy. The movement is repeated, the force is recharged and the energy is recycled at the same time. This is called the law of reversion. In this way, the internal alchemy system of Tai Chi movement expresses the principle of perpetual self-regeneration.

Most philosophies are merely intellectual concepts. However, Tao is not a concept and cannot be grasped conceptually. Taoist philosophy actually transcends the realm of philosophy because it can be clearly demonstrated through movement in daily life. Tai Chi movement reveals to us all of the profound cosmic principles expounded in Lao Tzu's *Tao Te Ching*. Lao Tzu frequently mentions the importance of avoiding fullness, because when the peak of fullness is reached, decline is inevitable. In Tai Chi movement we learn how to control our energy to avoid fullness, thereby avoiding the peaks of growth and decay.

One of the main goals in the practice of the Integral Way is to discover and embrace the undivided root (wu chi) of the universe. With daily practice of Tai Chi movement we may evolve to subtler and subtler levels of being and ultimately accomplish oneness with the Subtle Origin of all creation (Tao).

8 Macrocosm and Microcosm: The Universal Energy Net and Energy Organization in the Body

Macrocosm: The Universal Energy Net

The vibrational frequency of energy has its own specific channel whereby it is transmitted throughout the cosmos. All universal channels are interwoven, forming a subtle network which contains all existence within it. The mutual attraction of yin and yang energies throughout the entire universe creates the interweaving of this cosmic energy net. The universal energy network is somewhat similar to the vast and complex transportation system of a large modern city. Like the lanes of modern freeways, each energy channel has its own scope and range of activity. The channels of the subtle universal energy are omni-dimensional and resemble the ground states of electrons which orbit the nucleus of an atom.

If one violates the regulative order of an energy channel by violating cosmic law, the result is disharmony and dissolution. On the other hand, by following the natural order of the positive energy channels one may achieve harmony with the universe and manifest a healthy, fruitful life. Achieving harmony in one's life is like aiming an arrow at a target and precisely hitting the bull's eye. Discord, sickness and disaster are merely a matter of "missing the mark," or extending oneself beyond the appropriate course for one's own inherent nature.

The energy network of the universe is an inescapable net. If you touch a string of the energy net, you will get a response. If you insistently construct your own energy net by holding fast to your emotions, desires, attachments and ideas, you become like a silkworm which spins out a cocoon, only to imprison itself. However, if you can transcend your own mind, you can avoid being trapped in its net. Then, although you are still living within the vast universal energy network, you will enjoy freedom of action and being because of the understanding and ability which you achieved.

In order to hit the bull's eye of one's subtle target which is the essential core of one's being, one must project the arrows of one's thoughts and actions with accuracy so that they follow the correct energy channels. The true, appropriate course is held within our own natures, but we miss it in the confusion and distortion caused by mental conditioning. The course is obscured by our misunderstanding as a result of the incomplete development of our minds and spirits.

Before a human being enters the physical plane to become individualized, he or she resides in the cosmic womb of nature. In some respects this is analogous to the experience of being a fetus in the womb of one's physical mother. While contained within your mother's womb, you were one with her; whatever your mother experienced you also experienced. In the process of birth you became separated from your mother. Your direct connection with her was cut. Similarly, before being born into this plane, we were one with nature and thus with universal law. Yet when we take physical form, we appear to become separated from the cosmic mother; we seem to lose our oneness with the universe and its law. We see nature and universal natural law as separate and external to our own nature. In truth, this separation is only an illusion, but when we accept the illusion as true, we also accept the separation.

After being born into the physical plane, we must rediscover universal law and restore our innate spiritual ability. By so doing, we reestablish our direct connection with nature, the cosmic mother of the universe. The reason we are no longer one with universal law in the postnatal stage is that we individualize ourselves via the mind. We perceive everything in terms of subject and object. We see universal nature as something other than ourselves. Actually we are the universal energy and the universe is us. Now our sensitivity to the movement of the vast universe is limited because we have physical form. Yet we need only to break through the shell of the ego to realize that we are one with the universe and that our concepts of externality and separateness are simply perceptual errors.

The Universal Principle of Harmony, Order, and Balance

The universe is a model of supreme order, the perfection of which is beyond the ability of the mortal mind to arrange, imagine, or describe, although this attempt is made by many. The Earth revolves regularly on its axis, receiving the sun's rays only on the surface facing the sun at each moment, thus creating light and darkness, day and night.

With exquisite symmetry, each of the planets in the solar system follows its own course around the sun. Similarly, the negatively charged electrons orbit the positively charged nucleus of each atom.

Harmony is the subtle yet inviolable power of the universe, whereas force and violence are aberrations. This is fundamental universal law. Every positive manifestation in the universe comes forth as the result of the creative, harmonized union of yin and yang energies and each manifestation has its own unique energy arrangement and pattern of movement. Following the inherent order of the universe results in harmony and balance; opposing the cosmic principle of natural order creates destruction.

When artificial means are used, to split atoms for example, the natural order of the atom is violated and massive devastation as nuclear explosion is the result. Whenever humankind creates radical change by violating the laws of nature, the end result is destruction. There are times when nature herself creates radical change, and, although there may be destruction and a taking away of the old, there is also creation of new life. However, if artificial deviation from the state of universal order occurs, the principles of cosmic law immediately go into effect to rectify and balance the deviation, because disorder is against the true nature of the universe and therefore cannot last.

Everything created and everything as yet uncreated comes forth from the same Subtle Origin (Tao). And because everything in the universe shares the same original source, all of the parts of the universe share the same true nature as the whole, from the most minute atomic particle to the most vast and magnificent star. The true nature of the universe and thus that of every human being is creative, productive, progressive, orderly and harmonious. Aberrant thinking and behavior, that is, thinking and behavior which deviate from the natural universal moral order of harmony, balance, and productivity, will absolutely evoke a negative response from the corresponding universal energies, as surely as a shadow follows its form.

Since all of our behavior is an extension of what is held in the mind, it is necessary to set the mind in right order so that it contains only positive energy to be rightly manifested in our lives. Carefully choose your thoughts, emotional reactions and words; weed out those negative in nature because they will attract the negative energies of the same frequency which will manifest in your life as negative experience and harmful results. By engaging in constructive, creative activities which are beneficial not only to yourself but to others as well, you increase the interaction of the internal and external positive energies and thereby attract the response of the corresponding energies of the universe.

Whether or not one has set high spiritual goals for oneself, it is essential to thoroughly understand the principles of response and attraction of energy and to use it scrupulously because the success of both worldly life and spiritual growth depends upon such understanding. If it is one's spiritual goal to connect one's energy with that of the highest realms of the universe, the foundation upon which one's self-cultivation must be built is the principle of energy response.

The seeker of the deeper reality of life must have a strong, virtuous character and a sense of moral responsibility as a prerequisite to learning the subtle universal truths. To reform a selfish, ruthless person who goes against the universal laws of natural physics is to destroy a demon; to instruct an individual in a strong sense of moral responsibility and obedience to the subtle laws of life is to instruct him in becoming a divine being.

Universal law is absolute and impartial. It can be evaded by no one. The cosmic laws of energy are just as binding on sages as they are on ordinary individuals. Were they something one could adhere to today and escape tomorrow, they would be of no more consequence than our artificial man-made laws. The purpose of learning universal law is to gain self-mastery and peace. We lack tranquility in our lives because we have strayed from our true nature and lost our knowledge of universal law, which is not outside us but within. After all, individuals are the embodiment of universal law itself, manifesting as human beings.

If then we follow our true inner nature, we will be following universal law. The problems in our lives are generally not caused by seriously immoral behavior, but rather by our unconscious violation of the correct order of energy. Many people may be interested in spiritual disciplines or traditions, but without understanding the laws of energy, one will still manifest disharmony in one's life despite the acquisition of spiritual knowledge and techniques.

Despite the fact that transgressions against natural law may sometimes appear to go unnoticed by the universe, the fruits of the violations must inevitably be harvested. This cosmic law is just as impartial in the mental realm as is the law of gravity in the physical realm, and its influence is just as inescapable.

The Yin and Yang Principle in Behavior

In order to achieve harmony in one's behavior it is necessary to balance the yin and yang, to integrate the yin and yang as one unit again. For instance, it is not enough to develop wisdom and understanding. In spiritual learning, wisdom and understanding are considered yin qualities. to achieve only these without cultivating the yang energy to realize these qualities is to have one-sided development. Anything one-sided is incomplete.

The integral approach to personality development classifies some virtues as yin and some as yang. These need to be balanced. Patience is a good virtue to develop, and it is a yin or passive virtue. Progressiveness, a yang or active virtue, is also a desirable virtue to cultivate. Patience and progressiveness must stand to balance within one's personality. When yin and yang are combined, we have complete virtue. Incomplete virtue can cause disaster. Take kindness as an example. Without the application of intelligence, kindness, itself a cardinal virtue, would be only blind kindness which can do much damage. In the physical realm, nature demonstrates blind kindness by supporting poison ivy as well as beneficial plants. We must remember that a human being is not merely a manifestation of the physical aspect of the universe. He is rather a complete model of the universe, demonstrating the physical as well as mental and spiritual aspects of existence. Thus one must not only be kind, but intelligent as well, and vice versa.

The principle of yin and yang is also demonstrated in the realm of emotions. For example, sentiment is a yin type of emotion, while joy is a yang type; worry is yin, while anger is yang. All emotional elements should find moderate expression on appropriate occasions or one will destroy the normal balance of one's feelings.

An important point to remember is that the sage does not employ a strict dogmatism in the question of proper behavior. He rather takes a more empirically provable stance. By intelligently applying the principles of yin and yang, and by observing the efficacy of these truths, one is provided with a scientific tool for accomplishing specific desired results. With such a tool, one may achieve harmony and balance in all aspects of one's life.

Microcosm: Energy Organization in the Body

The study of the principles of the Integral Way invariably leads one to inquire into the art of acupuncture. As we come to understand that the spiritual process is one of harmonizing and refining one's physical, mental, and spiritual energy, it becomes important to know the mechanics of the energy system and its operation in the human body. One also needs to clearly understand that this knowledge of the oneness of the human body, mind and spirit was not obtained through dissecting the body and observing its anatomy as is the practice in western medical research. It may seem amazing, but the ancient spiritually achieved ones used their mental ability of clear and unimpeded vision and recognition to compile their knowledge of the energy circulation in the channel system of the human body. Even if one is not interested in spiritual evolution, it is valuable to understand the principles of energy within the body in order to maintain one's equilibrium and health, both physically and mentally.

Acupuncture, a facet of the integral healing system, is a precise science dealing with the processing, storage, distribution and functioning of vital energy within the human organism, and the relationship of this energy to the cosmos. Acupuncture affects the circulation of energy within the human being on an extremely subtle level. The ancient achieved ones discovered that there is a subtle energy manifestation circulating throughout the organs and flesh which ultimately permeates every tissue and cell of the body. The name given to this energy is qi which has been translated as "vital energy" or "life force." Human beings are the embodiment of all the energies of the universe, including the energies of the sun, moon and stars as well as the various energies of the Earth.

For thousands of years, the spiritually developed ones have had a clear understanding of the inseparability and dynamic interplay of man and nature. The energies embodied by an individual and the energies of the cosmos follow the same natural laws. Thus, the principles of yin and yang and the five phases of energy evolution operate within the human body, just as they do in the vast body of the cosmos, and their systematic symbolisms are likewise applied to the metaphysical medicine developed in ancient China.

The five phases of energy evolution have their corresponding internal organs: wood corresponds with the liver and gallbladder; fire corresponds with the heart, small intestine, pericardium and triple warmer; earth corresponds with the spleen/pancreas and the stomach; metal corresponds with the lungs and large intestine; water corresponds with the kidneys and bladder. The climatic conditions of the four seasons, including wind, rain, lightning, thunder and frost, also have their corresponding manifestations within the body. All of these transformations of bipolar energy interact within a human being, producing the life manifestations known as body, mind and spirit in their various expressions.

The 12 Main Energy Channels

The human body is a microcosm of the universe. Like a miniature universe, the cyclical and constant movement and transformation of fluids, molecules, cells, chemicals and energies within the body characterize life. As water springs forth from the deep earth and flows into streams and then rivers and finally the sea, the qi or life force traverses the body within tributaries and canals that we call channels. The 12 main channels each correspond to a particular organ. And not unlike the self-sustaining universe, the qi flows perpetually, filling the empty and draining the excess from parts of the body regulated by an intrinsic balancing mechanism. Therefore, the channels play an important role in the healthy functioning of human life.

The sages divided all of the channels into classifications of yin and yang based upon the polarization of energy within the body. All of the yang channels connect with organs involved in the intake and digestion of food, and with the excretive organs. All of the yin channels connect with the organs active in the transformation and storage of the energy obtained from food. Each channel carries the name of the organ it is primarily associated with. The twelve main channels are the channels of the energies of the organs, each of which may be classified in terms of yin and yang as well as through the five phases of energy evolution (see table below).

The 8 Extraordinary Energy Channels

There are eight extraordinary channels. These eight channels are called "extraordinary" because of their unique function and pathways. They function as reservoirs to store and release qi depending on the state of the 12 main channels. The most important of the eight extraordinary channels are the Governing (Du) and the Conception (Ren) channels that run along the midline in the back and front of the body respectively. The other 6 extraordinary channels are: the Vitality (Chong Mai) channel, the Belt (Dai Mai) channel, the Yang Connecting (Yang Qiao) channel, the Yin Connecting (Yin Qiao) channel, the Yang Regulating (Yang Wei) channel, and the Yin Regulating (Yin Wei) channel [need illustration for energy channels].

The Path of Qi Circulation

The following is the typical path of qi circulation. The stomach and spleen system produces nutritive qi by extracting the essence of food. From the middle warmer (middle jiao, in which the stomach/spleen have absorbed nutritive qi), post-natal qi is then transported to the Lung channel in the upper cavity. The energy transportation/circulation cycle starts with the Lung channel.

12 Main Channels	Yin or Yang	Energy Phase	Peak Time
1. Lung	yin	Metal	3 – 5 a.m.
2. Large Intestine	yang	Metal	5 – 7 a.m.
3. Stomach	yang	Earth	7 – 9 a.m.
4. Spleen	yin	Earth	9 – 11 a.m.
5. Heart	yin	Fire	11 – 1 p.m.
6. Small Intestine	yang	Fire	1 – 3 p.m.
7. Urinary Bladder	yang	Water	3 – 5 p.m.
8. Kidney	yin	Water	5 – 7 p.m.
9. Pericardium	yin	Fire	7 – 9 p.m.
10. Triple Warmer	yang	Fire	9 – 11 p.m.
11. Gall Bladder	yang	Wood	11 – 1 a.m.
12. Liver	yin	Wood	1 – 3 a.m.

This is according to the solar clock (which is not affected by daylight-saving time). The energy flow is a natural cycle that takes 24 hours to complete.

The Governing (Du) and Conception (Ren) channels are the two primary extraordinary channels. The Governing (Du) channel is the yang part of the energy cycle. The Conception (Ren) channel is the yin part of the energy cycle.

The energy or qi in the Governing (Du) channel circulates from 6:01 a.m. to 6:00 p.m., a 12-hour period, representing the yang, active phase of a human life. The energy or qi in the Conception (Ren) channel circulates from 6:01 p.m. to 6:00 a.m., the other twelve hours, representing the yin phase.

The front, yin channel, which is called the Conception or Bearing Channel (Ren Mei), has a negative polarity. The yang channel on the back, which is called the Governing Channel (Du Mei), has a positive polarity. When the qi of these two channels is flowing smoothly, all is well, so keeping them unblocked and clear is basic to all other practices.

The Conception or Bearing (Ren) Channel originates at the perineum (Sea Bottom Cavity) which is also called "Yin Intesection" in acupuncture. It ascends along the interior of the abdomen along the front midline to the throat and then curves around the lips, passes through the cheek and enters the infraorbital region (under the eyes). In cultivation, qi flows from the head to the perineum.

The Governing (Du) Channel also originates at the perineum but ascends up through the spinal column to DU 16 (directly below the external occipital protuberance) where it enters the brain. It then ascends to the crown of the head and winds down the forehead to the roots of the upper teeth.

These two channels are not connected at the top. When the tongue touches the roof of the mouth, the yin and yang channels are connected and the circuit is complete. We frequently touch the roof of our mouth with the tongue during everyday activities; however, in meditation (moving or sitting), a continuous circuit is important. The tongue should be relaxed; if it is tense, it can result in stagnation of qi. The tongue should not touch the teeth or the connection will not be effective, and one tends to become sleepy. The tongue also should not be stretched back too far or it will be tight and the qi will stagnate. The spot on the soft palate where the tongue touches is called "Heaven's Pond" (Tien Tzie) or "Dragon Spring" (Lung Chuan).

The Three Tan Tien

Let us discuss the tan tien, which are the three main energy centers of the body. A tan tien is an internal energy center located in a specific region of the body. In modern times, it could be called a nerve center. Many parts of the body can be a specific energy field. Thus, you can consider a tan tien to be everywhere, particularly in a person who is achieved and is able to gather energy anywhere he or she desires.

There are three tan tien in the human body. The upper tan tien is located inside the central point between the eyebrows. The middle tan tien is located inside the central point of the chest. The lower tan tien is inside the lower abdomen. When the concentration is focused on one of these areas, different effects are produced.

The term tan tien translates as "field of elixer," and refers more to an area than a point. These major energy storage areas of the body provide energy for the various expressions of one's being, specifically the intellectual, emotional and sexual aspects, which correspond to the upper, middle and lower tan tien, respectively. However, the energy stored in each of these locations can be refined through cultivation without indulging in these expressions.

As a rule, women are advised to keep their energy centered in the middle tan tien. This is because a woman's natural center is already low. For most people, especially women and young men (due to the strength of sexual energy associated with the lower tan tien), the middle tan tien is the right, safe spot to pay attention to and cultivate. Thus, after you finish practicing Tai Chi, and at other times of the day, you may wish to focus your energy at the heart center or middle tan tien.

The Purpose of Circulating Qi

Energy or qi circulates continuously through all the channels in the body, much like rivers and streams that nourish the land it touches. Within humans, the unique attribute of consciousness allows the opportunity to influence the flow of qi by mental conductance. To begin with, most people's qi is weak or stagnant, usually in cavities where the channels are more narrow or harder to penetrate. The purpose of circulating qi is to open areas of blockage and enable the qi to flow smoothly.

Why is keeping qi circulating critical? We merely have to look at the function of qi to understand why. Qi within humans is the same qi as that which pervades our universe and maintains the cyclic movements of the planetary bodies. In humans, qi is essential as the basis for life, movement, impetus, warmth, engine behind extraction of nutrients and disposal of waste, the electrical impulses of a thought, and catalyst behind all functions that are systemic and cellular. Simply put, life happens because of qi!

Our mind can influence qi circulation and the more we train our mind and our qi, the more responsive and powerful they become. Ultimately, when the mind and qi are in concert, there is harmony and health. When the mind and qi are disjointed, there is chaos and disease. In spiritual cultivation and achievement, strong mind, potent qi and good health are the essential ingredients.

The story of Great Yu illustrates the principles of properly circulating qi. Great Yu is considered the greatest civil engineer in Chinese history. Having lived four thousand years ago in the valley along the Yellow River of China, he and the civilization of China faced threats of extinction from the regular floods and droughts that would bring devastation to life-sustaining crop lands. Yu was a keen astronomer and student of Tao who observed the heavens and understood the laws of nature.

To solve this life-threatening problem, he devised the world's first elaborate network of canals, locks and reservoirs that were so effective, it ensured not only the survival but the subsequent positive development of the Chinese civilization. The network he built channeled off excess water during flood seasons into reservoirs, and ensured steady water supply for irrigation during drought seasons. The ingenious feat earned him the throne of Emperor and thus establishing his family as the first imperial dynasty of China called Shia. Acupuncture developed utilizing the same principles. Thus, it is not difficult to see the same principle applied to the human body in which qi within a network of channels need to be effectively managed for maximum benefit.

9 The Tai Chi Sword and Spiritual Swordsmanship

In governing one's life

    One learns not to be aggressive.

If force is used,

    Internal harmony is disturbed

    And self-destruction will follow.

It is not often worth it to fight over material gain.

The gentle way can always help you achieve your correct goal.

           - Lao Tzu[1]

Spiritual Swordsmanship and the Internal School

The school of spiritual swordsmanship has a long historical background. It began with the tradition of the Way and combined martial arts with spiritual practice. All students were trained this way to different degrees. They deepened the art and kept their purpose strictly secret. They worked to achieve one goal: to deter and thwart evil. Some government officials were powerful and malevolent. Such tyrants would receive an ultimatum from the spiritual swordsmen to improve their harmful behavior or be punished. This was done by Mo Tzu's descendants or spiritual heirs. Their way of fighting evil was similar to western chivalry and the tradition of the knight errant.

By the way, the word "school," as it was used in ancient times, refers to a group of people who share similar beliefs or a common goal. A school was not a formal classroom situation like today's schools.

A spiritually achieved person in the School of Internal Swordsmanship could use his achieved mind to decapitate an officer who was a hundred or a thousand miles away. That kind of power is described in Chinese literature, but such a thing cannot be proven.

In the beginning, chivalrous swordsmen came from Mo Tzu's school. Later, the School of Spiritual Swordsmanship of Master Lu Tung-Ping and Master Zhang San-Feng followed the moral discipline of Mo Tzu and developed further to include physical movement, which could be converted into martial arts.

Now we follow all true sages who teach courage and who help the world through spiritual development. However, some people who learn spiritual development have a different understanding of worldly problems. No one should adopt the practice of killing anyone out of righteousness. The existence of evil in politics is due to two things: first, systems of monarchy and dictatorship, and second, the lack of individual development. The solution to bad government lies in education, not killing. The solution to the lack of personal development is obviously spiritual cultivation. Good self-government is the best foundation for social government. Thus, the focus of the spiritual practice of swordsmanship has changed to include teaching people how to be spiritual knight errants instead of social radicals who take extreme action.

Transforming your own evil, not killing other people, is the only thing that can transform the world. In the first place, it is neither our responsibility nor our privilege to judge others. The enjoyment of killing is a symptom of spiritual undevelopment. Thus, if you wish to help the world, do it through developing yourself first and then through spiritual teaching, not through killing.

Moral courage is nurtured by gentle physical movement, which gives you confidence in yourself. The training and preparation to become a teacher of spiritual swordsmanship is the same as that for the martial arts. The only difference is in the way the goal is achieved. There is no doubt that the world needs help from capable people. Those who wish to offer help through spiritual and peaceful means must have the moral courage of knights of old. Those who act in what looks like evil ways simply do not understand the subtle part of life and need to develop themselves more.

Actually, if you were to kill someone whom you think is an evil person, you would kill only the body; the energy cannot be killed. Rather than trying to kill something that can't be killed, we need to improve and change any environment that fosters the growth of evil. Thus, it is better to leave the body of a so-called evil doer alive, and work in positive ways toward transforming the sociocultural environment. This is the new direction of the school of the spiritual swordsman. For this purpose, a new type of martial art and weapon exercises were developed.

The Power of the Invisible Sword Is the Power of Your Own Spirit

Certain physical practices can be used to attain spiritual development, however, if you learn the skills but not the spirit, then you are not yet a student of the School of Spiritual Swordsmanship. This is why we are careful when we teach the skill. At the same time, we need to point out the direction or goal of its origin, which is to help other people develop themselves spiritually.

Thank you for your interest in learning this art. Always remember that it is only for your self-protection. You do not have the right to judge others and use the skill against them.

The Spiritual Power of the Sword

When I (OmNi) was practicing Traditional Chinese Medicine in Taiwan, I taught Tai Chi movement. At that time, Tai Chi was taught as a martial art. If you are in the business of teaching martial arts and wish to attract students, you need good achievement or no one will recognize you as a teacher. I was doing quite well in martial arts, but my livelihood came from my medical practice.

One day, an older student who came from northeastern China brought a precious sword from his hometown. It had belonged to someone else, and he had received it as a gift. He was the manager of a big factory who had good business training. I taught him internal Qigong to increase his health, and he gave the sword to me as a gift. I protected it well, but it still needed some special care to prevent it from becoming rusty.

One noon, I wished to clean the sword, so I pulled it from its sheath. I should not have done that at noontime, but I was busy, and that was the only free time I had. The sheath was hard to remove, so I needed to use some force to take the sword out. I pulled out the sword, a big rat who was hurt by this somewhat intense energy fell down from the ceiling. It had died on the spot and had no apparent wound in its body. It was hurt by the energy. Friends jokingly described the rat as the evil spirit that happened to hide in my ceiling wishing to steal my energy.

This experience proved to me that the mythology of a good sword's spiritual power is possible. Because I do not have any enemies, my sword has never killed anybody, but that occasion proved that the sword has spiritual power. The sword is power, and the power is a sword.

I gave that sword to a student before I left Taiwan, because such a thing could not be taken out of the country. I hope he is still taking good care of it.

Many stories have been told about precious swords. Some were said to jump down from the wall on which they hung to respond to their master and kill an enemy, or they would make a noise to warn of intruders.

The higher level of spiritual sword was not made of metal, but of personal spiritual energy. Such a sword could kill evil and protect its master's personal spiritual essence.

The School of Spiritual Swordsmanship

Master Lu Tung-Ping of the Tang Dynasty (618-906 C.E.), and Master Zhang San-Feng who came after him, both achieved the art and virtue that belonged to the School of Spiritual Swordsmanship. They also belonged to the School of Golden Immortal Medicine which is the practice of internal and external alchemy[2].

The School of Spiritual Swordsmanship and the School of Golden Immortal Medicine are both heritages of the Integral Way. The internal school is an entirely spiritual practice. It is different from the external school, which develops physical energy for fighting. The ancient sages used physical movement to guide students to learn the limitation of physical strength, and thus lead them into spiritual practice.

Physical movement is a tool for spiritual training. Because spirit itself has no form or shape, it cannot be controlled without a certain physical form, shape or movement. For most people, spiritual practice is just the practice of mind through reading, recitation, chanting or prayer. Generally, they do not consider that spiritual practice comes through being. Whatever you do, you become. Thus, doing any of the gentle movements is more beneficial and direct than praying. Prayer is external, because a person prays to external beings, by chanting or reciting a sutra or whatever. The Integral Way goes directly to your life being and is directly involved with your life movement.

The Sword and Spiritual Cultivation

New generations continue the spirit of the Spiritual Swordsman by accepting the invisible sword as a metaphor for cultivating and refining their spirit. Let us explain further.

In Chinese culture, the materials used to make a sword need to go through a long process. A great quantity of pig iron must be refined to produce the quality of steel fit for a sword. In ancient times, a sword was usually made by using water and fire. Metal was heated in the fire, shaped, and then put into water to be cooled. This process was repeated over and over again. It took many repetitions to make a sword so refined and sharp that it could split a hair, and making a sword turn out well required great spiritual attention. It was not a simple procedure, sometimes it took years. Some swords were so finely made that they were not only very sharp, but were also very flexible. They could be bent back or curved, but when released would return to their original straightness.

This process is similar to the process of spiritual cultivation. The development of human spirits is similar to the process of alternating heat and cold. Through the heat of fire and cold of water, a person's soul becomes firm and right to the point. The water and the fire in a person's life are the troublesome circumstances and experiences through which one learns to improve oneself and develop an indestructible and undefeatable character.

Spiritual swordsmanship is not based on the sharpness of cutting with a physical sword, but upon the greater power of righteousness and harmony. This again describes the difference between the internal and external schools.

The Attainment of Spiritual Refinement

When I (OmNi) was a teenager, most people in China did not like to leave their home town. However, an elder encouraged me to do so. He said, "If you wish to face the entire world, your hometown is not the place to stay. Only by meeting trials and ordeals will you become mature. A person of the Way makes all towns his home, all nations his nation and all people his kin. The way to achieve oneself in the Way is by first learning to give up all easily obtained support from others, then to create your own life by meeting all possible difficulties. The strongest spirit can only be realized by going through the overly heated fire and overly cold ice of life circumstances. If one can rise above them, one has mastered life."

When I was young, I was not smart enough to be a student of spiritual immortality. Instead, I was attracted by physical arts and the great swordsmen in stories. It was not until later that I deeply appreciated the type of spiritual swordsmanship described by Chuang Tzu in his story of the butcher who used his knife for nineteen years without sharpening it. It had no nicks or dents because of the butcher's refinement and skill in the use of the blade. That was a great education.

Refinement is something that we need to learn and use in our daily lives. This is especially true today because of the interdependence of many elements of modern life. People live by supporting one another. A cooperative spirit and a willingness to help are needed.

The reward of teaching is the spiritual development of all people. My spiritual teaching comes from my achievement in swordsmanship, while my teaching of physical arts is from my spiritual learning. My private joy is practicing the arts.

Spiritual Swordsmanship and Health

Once I (OmNi) had an interesting experience. I got a cold, but I could not stop seeing patients because the appointments were already made. I was suffering from the cold and sat in my chair in the early morning. My vision started acting; I saw myself doing some sword dancing. Suddenly, I understood that doing sword dancing was the cure for my cold. So I did the sword dancing to force the virus out by a little sweating, got over the suffering and went back to work.

Similar inspiration comes to me, for my work, writing or other activities. A positive, busy minded person can always receive spiritual help if he is quietly listening for it. The attitude of rushing and haste always slows down the expected good harvest. All teachings given were also received in the same way.

PART THREE:
TAI CHI PRACTICE

10 Guidelines for Practicing Tai Chi Chuan

A young man traveled to a foreign land to attend the school of a famous teacher of Tao. When he arrived at the school he was interviewed by the teacher.

"What do you wish from me?" the teacher asked.

"I wish to be your student and become the finest Taoist in all the land," the man replied. "How long must I study?"

"A minimum of twenty years," the teacher answered.

"Twenty years is a long time," said the young man. "What if I studied twice as hard as all your other students?"

"Forty years," was the teacher's reply.

"Why is that?" the puzzled young man asked.

"When one is fixated on the achievement, the mind becomes tight and one is further from the Way than before," responded the teacher.

INTRODUCTION

In doing Tai Chi movement and in living our lives, our goal is to be healthy and normal. Nothing special, just normal. The movement in Tai Chi practice is a constant, healthy flow, not an erratic flow that is subnormal or abnormal.

Part of living a healthy, spiritual life includes being active in the morning and reposeful in the evening. A healthy schedule is good for your practice as well as for your health and overall well-being. Do those things that are of lasting benefit rather than short-lived advantage or immediate gratification.

A practitioner of self-cultivation practices endurance under pressure and maintains balance when there is no trouble. Therefore, an achieved one, like the center of the universe, is inexhaustible.

Our goal is to fully achieve ourselves while living within the inescapable network of worldly life. Other spiritual traditions claim that liberation means giving up worldly life to live as a hermit in the forests or as a beggar in the streets. That kind of liberation is only a futile attempt to escape from life. Life is an inescapable network in which everyone is involved. True freedom from difficulties, be they conceptual, spiritual or physical, cannot be found in an artificial lifestyle. A truly achieved person is someone whose spirit is free, whatever the circumstances of life happen to be; in other words, a healthy person who is able to rise above passing troubles that have no real importance.

Doing Tai Chi is so simple. When we describe it intellectually it may sound complicated, but that is not the reality. When you truly practice a gentle physical art such as Tai Chi movement, it is not just an exercise, it is life. In life, each movement and each action expresses the same integral truth that Tai Chi movement embodies and expresses. Nothing can separate you or your actions from that truth.

How to Use Tai Chi

When practicing Tai Chi to achieve complete health in the three spheres (your body, mind and spirit), keep in mind the following general guidelines.

Use Harmony Style Tai Chi (or its equivalents) to untie the tensions and knots in your body that result from your emotions.

Use Tai Chi to soften your personality, especially if you are overly tight due to a fear of being beaten by others. The tightness you feel is usually a result of not feeling completely confident with yourself.

Use the practice to increase the flexibility of your body, mind and spirit, and as the path of self-development. For example, you can use the practice for your general healthcare, and thereby reduce the risk of modern medical abuse. Or you could use Tai Chi to help heal a chronic illness. People lacking self-control usually don't understand these things.

More importantly, use Tai Chi for spiritual self-cultivation, self-attunement in worldly life and the refinement of your personality. Also use Tai Chi to access the deep levels of your being, such as the chi level of life, the jin level of application, and the Shen level of the final reality.

GENERAL INSTRUCTION

Where to Practice

It is suitable to do this exercise in a park or your own back or front yard, as long as there is no distraction from nearby roads, thick dust, or people. Any quiet, undisturbed natural place is suitable for internal energy cultivation. It is also all right to practice indoors with the windows open for fresh air.

In China, many older people practice Tai Chi every morning in the parks. We encourage our friends to offer such a service in this country as well. Usually there is no charge for such a class, it is a pure service. Some of our students charge for each class.

When to Practice

You might practice in the early morning before breakfast. Most people go to work after that, but if you already have material support and you have the chance, you might practice again later in the day. If you are an early bird and get up at 4:00 a.m., you can practice then. The later hours are for people with a different schedule.

For people who do mental work, the best time to exercise is from three to five o'clock in the afternoon, but not after five. Exercise about forty minutes before dinner, and then eat a light dinner. Do not overdo it in the morning either.

Physical law and the law of the mind are the same. For example, if you spend a lot of time thinking in the evening, it is hard to stop thinking when you sleep. Similarly, doing vigorous physical movement and then immediately sitting down is too rapid a change and can be damaging to the lungs and other organs because of the sudden internal pressure that has gathered.

When you exercise in the morning, start very slowly and gently and then build up to a suitable speed later, but do not overly excite the body's energy either in the morning or at night.

Generally speaking, modern people do not have time to learn Tai Chi in the morning. They can learn in the evening, from a teacher, but personal practice is most beneficial in the early morning. Dawn is a very beneficial time, energy-wise. The amount of time it takes to make progress varies from person to person. It is a very individual thing. For some people it takes many years, while for others the amount of time is shorter.

All achieved teachers, whether they teach martial arts or personal health and longevity, get up early in the morning.

Because most people work so hard in the daytime and sleep so late, we suggest that they not overdo it. We believe that twenty minutes will be good enough.

When you do Tai Chi Exercise, do not do it too fast or too slow. Tai Chi Movement itself is energy conducting. Maybe you are sleepy in the morning. If you do it too fast, you will have too much energy all day. It is like, when you drink a glass of water, you control its temperature so that it is neither too hot nor too cold. You are the one doing the Tai Chi practice, so how fast and how long you do it depends entirely on what is most beneficial for you. You can always adjust it. Each day is different. Generally, around fifteen or twenty minutes is good enough. In the afternoon, around 4:00 or 5:00, if you do it once more for twenty minutes before the evening meal, that is good enough.

How Much to Practice

We do not think there should be a limitation on the amount of practice each day, because practice is how people achieve themselves. If somebody achieves less, it is because the interest is different. The amount of time you spend practicing is an individual matter; you should learn and practice according to your own opportunities and needs.

I (OmNi) do not approve of families who shut their young sons or daughters in the garden and make them practice Tai Chi for eight or ten hours a day. I have heard that some members of the Chen family do 20 to 40 repetitions of the same simple formula. With that kind of fervor, they may achieve a certain level in fighting, but I have never heard that anyone in the Chen family has ever lived to be a hundred years old.

Each person has their own natural internal clock. You know how long is right for you. I (OmNi) do it rhythmically. That means sometimes I do one form, stop, and then do another form. Sometimes I exercise for 20 minutes with music, then sometimes I continue with no music.

The main principle in whatever you do is to do it for enjoyment, not for external reasons. If you force yourself to do it, it will bring no benefit. If you do it for enjoyment, then you become a shien, which is a happy spiritual individual. That is the goal. Enjoyment comes from avoiding suffering. Do not create suffering for yourself by letting your mind betray your kingdom of life.

Posture and the Spine

We would like to share some special details on how to practice the physical arts. First, the spine should always be aligned, from the tailbone to where it joins the head, so that it is straight but not rigid like a drill instructor's posture. There should be a natural flexibility in its alignment. In some movements, the head is raised a little bit in order to adjust one's balance.

The internal school calls the spine "the dragon bone," or "the dragon," because it is the source of one's mental, physical and spiritual strength and also the means of communication between what is substantial and what is insubstantial. If the spine is not well aligned, the qi that flows through it moves poorly and one's health declines, because the powerful dragon is no longer active. A healthy spine is similar to the shape of a released or slightly pulled bow.

There is a second detail to be remembered. The tailbone, including the sphincter muscle around the anus, should always be tucked forward. Also, the chin should also be kept tucked in. The head needs to be kept erect, as if a string were attached to the top, pulling it up. Please remember all of this important knowledge. Your spinal alignment will sustain your internal energy flow.

If the body's posture and alignment are poor, the flow of qi becomes blocked and defeats the whole purpose of gentle movement. The important thing to remember when you learn good posture is to practice it at every moment of your life.

Center of Gravity

The mid point of the human body is the lower tan tien, which is located just below the navel. This should be your center of gravity, the place from which your movements originate when practicing most qi exercises. The three tan tien are also called the "Three Origins" (see Chapter 8).

The movements of Tai Chi are done in a standing position, thus it has a different requirement and purpose than sitting cultivation. Sitting meditation has its center of gravity in the middle tan tien, the heart area. Keeping your center in the lower tan tien strengthens both your physical and sexual stamina. However, please do not practice Tai Chi movement just to increase your sexual pleasure. Do it for your health.

Sexual strength is the source of physical health and longevity. A person whose sexual energy dies off at an early age cannot live to be very old. Do not rush into lots of sexual activity; not because you do not have the desire for it, but so that you can guard that energy and use it throughout your life. The sexual energy generated by Tai Chi movement improves your internal circulation and enhances all aspects of your life.

Be Clear In Mind

Develop mental clarity and do not emphasize individual movements. Tai Chi is an integral set of movements that are not discrete. It requires smoothness and completeness to weave all the pieces together in an integral whole.

Your mind should be passively active when you practice so you can be clear and precise about the message you are sending to your body. When your mind is garbled, like a computer with its memory in random places, you cannot be very clear in your commands, and your commands cannot be responded to with precision and speed. Thus, first you have to unclutter your mind so that you can focus. This is what it means to be passively active.

There is no need for imagery. Just watch what you are doing and unite the mind with the body. The mind is not your thinking, but your awareness.

Unification is the Integral Way.

Visualization is an internal exercise, and movement is an external exercise. Visualization can achieve the purpose on a subtle level, because the energy listens to the mind.

In some Qigong practices, particularly religious Qigong, there are different types of visualization that can be therapeutic for people who have a lot of illusions. If your mind is sick, that type of practice can be beneficial. However, pure concentration is better than complicated visualizations, although the purpose of both is the same.

In general, there is no moment when your mind is not active, whether you are awake or sleep. If the mind goes its own way, your "house" is left unattended or haunted by scattered memories. Spiritual cultivation can unify your three partners: body, mind and spirit.

Relax and Let the Energy Grow

During Tai Chi Chuan practice, it is not helpful to think about combat or fighting with somebody. Just do it as a pure energy exercise. This peace will become supportive in nuturing your energy. If you have any other thoughts during your Tai Chi practice, then your Tai Chi practice is not helpful. Once you are doing all right, the energy itself will grow naturally. Like our ancestors, you will feel as though you are bathing in a warm spring breeze. You feel so good because your energy is producing, affecting. This kind of nice feeling is a result or an experience of one's own cultivation. It is not artificial, something caused by taking a drug to make you feel good. Drugs do harm to a person. But Tai Chi Chuan is a true way to nurture your true energy. When qi comes to a certain part of the body, you feel it. For example, if you bring the qi to your head, you might feel as though you have a thousand ants scratching or that you have some itching on the skin of the head. It is not a bad feeling; it is a very pleasant feeling, difficult to describe. This kind of happiness, joy and pleasant feeling is the high condition of the harmony of the union of your life being, and all elements now put together produce the best energy for you.

The Tai Chi Principle

The cosmic tai chi principle is that of rhythmic alternation or movement. For example, inhaling and exhaling, or moving inward to collect energy in the center before moving outward from the center to the limbs. Most of you already understand the concept of yin and yang as two poles of all things. The cosmic tai chi principle is simply the alternation of these two forces.

The special term for the tai chi principle is "yin yang kai huh." Yin and yang can be translated as contraction and expansion. "Kai" means openness and "huh" means to close back. Thus, "kai huh" actually means the same thing as "yin yang."

If you learn the principle of "yin yang kai huh," then you know the most important guideline for how to do things and how to apply your strength or mind in all aspects of life, including business. Everything follows a pattern of rhythmic alternation. There is so much theory about this, but the reality never changes.

More interesting than talking or reading about the theory is experiencing the reality by practicing these ancient movements which have been developed and refined by generations of devoted practitioners. Doing them will broaden your understanding more than reading ten thousand books. They are all gentle movement, but the energy of each is quite different.

Tai Chi and Diet

A light diet, both in quality and quantity is most beneficial for practicing Tai Chi. Don't eat too much bread or rice or other heavy foods. Serious qi students usually eat very light foods like Chinese porridge, which is also called rice soup. It is easily digested, so you have time to do Tai Chi again. If you eat regular foods until you have a full belly, it will take four hours to digest it and you will not have time to do Tai Chi any more, because then it is time for your next meal. Instead, eat light foods in small amounts. This will be beneficial to your practice.

Sometimes I (OmNi) feel I eat too much because I enjoy gourmet food, but it is too difficult to do Tai Chi if you are interested in gourmet food. If you are really devoted to Tai Chi, maybe you can keep one day a month to enjoy gourmet food during a certain season. However, whether you eat simple food or gourmet food, do not practice Tai Chi on a full stomach.

Tai Chi Practice and Illness

If you are ill with a cold or the flu, for example, you should totally relax. Do not do Qigong or meditation or Tai Chi. A cold is a sign for you to rest. It is not necessarily an illness, but it is good to drink some warm herb tea.

Tai Chi and Older People

People who are physically weak or aging fast would greatly benefit from doing Gentle Path Tai Chi. When you are older, you have less vitality. Exercise increases vitality, and the value of Gentle Path is rejuvenation.

A person who is 50 years is not very old and is still young, and a young person has the potential to learn anything that is suitable. They need to start slowly and gently, and practice regularly. Someone who is 60, 70, or 80 can still start to exercise with Tai Chi. That is middle-age; we mean before 80. But we recommend starting earlier so that people can learn something that would make them more physically independent than relying on medication or a doctor and abandoning their natural potential for a long and happy life.

The School of Internal Harmony usually teaches gentle movement, so a trained teacher or trained individual knows to go in gradual steps with older people rather than big leaps.

The amount of time an older person practices each day is not a matter of age, but of how much the exercise affects them. If someone walks one mile he might be tired, but another person might walk a couple of miles and still be fresh. It depends on the individual.

When you start exercising, stop before you feel exhausted. A little tiredness is okay, such as when you climb a steep slope and begin to pant. Just do not over exert yourself. Gradually build yourself up through gentle movement. Be relaxed when you do it. Tension is what kills you, not gentle, graceful movements.

There is always a common factor, whatever a person's age, but there are also some differences. Discuss this with a really achieved teacher; they will know what is good for you. If you study with a teacher who only promotes one thing, you will never learn the truth of what is good for you.

Tai Chi and Self Defense

You cannot learn self-defense from martial arts alone. The best self-defense is the spiritual philosophy of being like a hen rather than a rooster. If you study martial arts for a long time, it may cause you to become too confident and think you are the strongest man in the world. This can cause you to push yourself to the verge of peril.

We only recommend martial arts as a spiritual cultivation, whether Shao Lin (the hard) or Wu Tang (the soft). This is the general way Chinese people distinguish them, as hard or soft. The Shao Lin School originally taught martial arts for spiritual purposes, but unfortunately it has become degraded into a tradition of combat. Wu Tang, which developed in the Wu Tang Mountains was Master Zhang San-Feng's tradition. He got the idea from Master Chen Tuan's concept of Tai Chi. Thus, Wu Tang has a more clear spiritual tradition, which we prefer.

Martial arts skills are just a side effect of constant practice. Many Tai Chi students show off fighting skills that are not derived from actual Tai Chi practice. They do something in addition to Tai Chi that does not prolong their life. Do not equate Tai Chi Chuan with martial arts. Chinese martial arts originated with Dao-In[1], which are internal conducting exercises whose truth and value lie in the exercise of qi. It is this exercise of qi which enables Tai Chi to increase physical and emotional balance and spiritual happiness.

Once you learn the form, you should study the *I Ching*[2] and the *Tao Te Ching*[3]. Tai Chi Chuan is just one way to practice the principles given in both of these great books. It is foolish to get involved in the different schools of martial arts. In learning Tao, the School of Internal Harmony is the correct way to increase your inner qi.

Tai Chi and Men

Men should be aware that with regular practice they will go through a stage of expanding their sexual energy, which, unfortunately, most tend to release through fighting and sex. Your training and attainment in Tai Chi should not be applied regressively; it should support your spiritual development. Therefore practice Tai Chi for self-control, rather than letting yourself be pulled into worldly affairs that are against the constructive direction of life. Women who possess an overabundance of testosterone may also benefit from this suggestion.

Tai Chi and Women

Gentle Path Tai Chi works with the center of gravity below the waist (see Chapters 14 and 20). It gives a solid foundation that can take you in any direction you may wish to go: martial arts, physical health or spiritual development.

A woman's center is already low. Women can practice Gentle Path, but they should not squat or bend too low. We recommend that women focus on the middle tan tien as their foundation. Because Sky Journey Tai Chi is in the middle range of speed and height, it is suitable (see Chapters 14 and 21). This exercise is adaptable to all kinds of people. Men and women of all ages can safely cultivate the middle tan tien.

Important Points to Remember Before Doing Any Style of Tai Chi

1. Relax! This is perhaps the most important principle in Tai Chi. Most of us tend to hold tension in various parts of the body, such as the shoulders and lower back. As you move, check the entire body for tension. Wherever you find tension, simply relax and release it. This will help you move more smoothly and freely. This is also a good principle for your life.

2. Move the whole body as a single unit. No part of the body moves in isolation from the whole. All movements are integrated and connected.

3. All moves originate in your feet, find direction in your waist, and are expressed in your arms and hands. Think of the movements like waves rippling through your body.

4. Be solid and rooted in your feet and light in your arms and head. Is your head over your body in line with your perineum?

5. Expand your back and sink your chest slightly.

6. Each move expands or contracts your entire torso.

7. Move slowly and naturally. This will allow you to look carefully inside yourself for any incorrect or unbalanced movements. Gradually cultivate stability and moderation in the movements.

8. Your mind should be quiet and concentrated. This will help focus your intent in doing the movements. Do not use muscular force.

9. When you are first learning the form, do not be concerned about coordinating your breathing with the movements. Just breathe naturally. Your breathing should be deep and diaphragmatic, keeping your lower abdomen relaxed.

10. Once you have learned the movements, you may try to coordinate the movements with your breathing, but do not take a rigid approach. Generally, as your hands rise or pull back toward the body, breathe in; as the hands descend or push away from the body, breathe out.

11. The tip of your tongue touches the upper palate.

12. Relax the shoulders and drop the elbows.

13. Relax the lower back and tuck in the lower part of the pelvis.

TWELVE PRINCIPLES OF TAI CHI PRACTICE AND DAILY LIFE

Gracefulness of Body and Spirit

The word "graceful" is generally used as an adjective, but it can be more than just a word in the dictionary, it can be a description of your life. You can cultivate gracefulness by practicing any of the forms of Qigong and Tai Chi.

No force is used in practicing gentle qi exercises. Qi moves, qi speaks and qi sings a natural, sweet and happy melody. You can express its melody of natural transformation through your movements and your life.

Try to do all your movements in a gentle manner. Do not thrash around. Relax. It is a gentle process of moving qi through the body. If you do anything abruptly, you can block the flow and end up with a headache or some other discomfort.

Evenness and Fullness

There is a special requirement called "jung yun yuan mang." "Jung yun" means evenness, with nothing sticking out, nothing unusual. Even if you place special emphasis on a certain movement, that movement will not "stick out" to an external observer.

"Yuan mang" means fullness. To be full means the whole body, from the tan tien to the finger, from the soles of your feet even to the tip of your hair, is full of energy.

Together, the phrase means that full development is attained through movement.

Naturalness

In all your movements, whether as exercise or in daily life activities, the key to success is naturalness. Nothing about these exercises is artificial or superficial. They are all deeply related to your natural physiological structure and how your energy flows through that structure.

Each movement of Tai Chi describes a circle. There are no abrupt or radical changes in direction, speed or style. You just keep making circles: small ones, large ones, horizontal, vertical or slanted ones, in all directions. All movements can be considered as one movement, because they are all connected. Whether you reach out or gather back, the pattern is cyclical. Some circles are too small to observe, but energy-wise they are a whirlpool.

The ancient achieved ones learned that there is no way that we can fight our own nature. For example, can you use your ear as a mouth to eat? No, you cannot. Can you use your eye to breathe? No, you cannot. Nature is nature. You have to learn to be compliant with nature regarding the basics. No one needs to think about being natural. Even without the conscious mind, the body responds harmoniously to most situations.

We cannot go against the nature of the universe. For example, if you sow seeds in winter with the intent of harvesting in spring, nothing will grow. Today, people use greenhouses, and by controlling light, temperature, and water they can make things grow. Nevertheless, even greenhouses are subject to natural limitations.

The ancient, gentle exercises illustrate cosmic principles and can bring one into great harmony with cosmic law as they guide and conduct one's internal energy. Cosmic law is important for personal internal harmonization, because each individual life is a small model of the universe.

The original gentle qi exercises are the result of the spiritual achievement and natural minds of sages who wished to maintain the wholeness of their spirit. Tai Chi movement is a natural movement that imitates the stars and galaxies that move around us and the internal movement inside each life. Today these same exercises can still help people return to naturalness.

Be Simple

Simplicity is important in spiritual cultivation. You might think that Tai Chi movement is not simple, but it teaches you to govern complexity with simplicity. The Way also teaches you to govern complex situations with the refined simplicity of your spirit. The principle of simplicity can be learned by doing Tai Chi movement, but it is not Tai Chi movement. The principle of simplicity can be applied to all situations in your life and business. A big company, a big government and the world itself can be understood and managed by simplicity. Simplicity is effective. If you engage in complications, you lose yourself. Learn to be simple.

Be Gentle

It is important to learn to be gentle and non-violent in speech, thought, emotion or action. Wise people know that treating others violently is the same as treating themselves violently. In Tai Chi movement, you can learn to be gentle. To be simple and gentle in daily life is one manifestation of the Integral Truth.

Be Unassertive and Non-Dominating

Be unassertive and non-dominating. Reality is always in the process of change. You only need to respond correctly to a changing situation. No situation is static, so no prearranged response will be effective. Ordinary people have preconceptions about life having to be a certain way, so they become nervous and act prematurely, which only makes the situation worse and causes real damage to other people and themselves.

Be Balanced and Poised

The next principle is to be balanced and poised in movement. You might think that is easy, but we don't think so. For example, even if a person sits still, is he calm and poised? Many people cannot even sit still. In Tai Chi movement, you learn the principle of balance and poise.

Be Calm

Learn to be calm, especially in rough situations. The flow of Tai Chi movement is calm. Most Qigong movements also follow this principle. Some styles of Qigong or martial arts may be vigorous, but a violent force never lasts for long.

Be Kind to All

Be kind to all beings. Tai Chi movement is not damaging or harmful in any way.

Be Frugal

The principle of frugality relates to daily life as much as to qi exercise. It is important to be frugal with regard to attachment to material objects, but abundant in gathering your energy. Both in daily life and in qi practice, you should protect your vital force and be frugal in using it. Do not be overly confident in using your physical, material and mental strength, but be prepared and make your practice a great source of energy provision for yourself. Be unattached to victory. Be frugal in the use of energy. Be rich in energy preparation or gathering. Make sure you always have enough energy to handle all situations.

Learn from gentle qi exercise and from the yin/yang principle (the cosmic tai chi principle) how to use your life force in a rhythmic pattern. Yin and yang means there is day and night in which you experience movement and quietness. If your hand stretches out, you must draw it back. If you kick your leg high, it must come down. Before you can jump high, you must first learn to crawl. If there is a left side, there must be a right side. If you have a front, you must have a back. You must take care of the whole thing, not just go forward without ever retreating, or walk to the left and never go right. Alternation and rhythmic movement are the principle of yin and yang. Do not overextend yourself in any of the Tai Chi movements or in anything you do in your life. Be frugal with your energy, and use this helpful principle in your daily life.

Know Where to Use Energy

Another principle of Tai Chi practice is to know the right time and place to use your energy so that your strength is applied efficiently to activities that are righteous and just.

This brings us to the next principle, which is smoothly avoiding a possible confrontation. Be unwilling to proceed with foolish action. Tai Chi movement never confronts force; you always yield. In daily life, this means not seeking profit or gain for unworthy or evil purposes. The purpose of this yielding is not to yield just for the sake of yielding, but to avoid confrontation and still be a winner.

Be Centered

Let us use Tai Chi Chuan exercise to illustrate the principle of "chung" or being centered. When in Tai Chi practice you utilize your strength, you must always be centered and able to keep your balance. If you over-use your strength, you have already lost your balance, then if you add even a little bit of strength to the direction in which you are going, certainly you will fall over. To practice Tai Chi movement is to learn how to make all movements properly and correctly from one's own supportive and reliable position. It is not to look for an opportunity to conquer others. It is not to be forceful or fierce looking or aggressive. The secret of winning depends on your correct movement. Tai Chi Chuan practice is not meant to practice for a fight; it is the training of the principle of properness in all ordinary life. In life or in Tai Chi practice, following those principles means that rather than fight, you give yourself tremendous room and freedom in movement.

EIGHT GUIDELINES FOR A HEALTHY AND BALANCED LIFE

The ancient Taoist spiritual teachings are rich in knowledge and techniques for the arrangement and development of a human's energy. Through the use of cultivation, a man or woman can serve oneself and others. Practitioners of the Integral Way refine their energy until it becomes as subtle as the pivotal energy of the universe. Any self-cultivation method applied at the appropriate time and in the appropriate place will cause the appropriate enduring result. In this way an achieved one practices the propriety of the natural Way of life as a balanced and fully developed universal being.

The simple life style consists of many fundamental practices. The easiest and most important practices are early rising and retiring, the practice of serenity in sitting and moving, heeding one's words, the avoidance of excessive sexual activity and indulgence in foods, and the abstinence from engagement in unnecessary activities. Each aspect is significant in the refinement of one's energy and needs to be attended to conscientiously and consistently.

1. Early Morning Cultivation

The very early morning is the best time for self-cultivation. This time affords one deep peace and quiet before the daily activities begin, and also enables one to gather the beneficial, tranquil energies which are available only during the very early morning hours. This practice enhances one's health as well as one's spiritual growth. Spending time outdoors among the energies of the trees and other plants early in the morning is revitalizing and calming to one's entire being.

2. Retire Early

Retiring before ten o' clock at night enables one to rise early. Five to six hours sleep each night are sufficient for an adult; too much sleep will cause stagnation in the body's energy flow. Sleeping in a sitting position or in one of the sleeping postures for spiritual cultivation enables one to accumulate subtle energy while sleeping[4].

3. Quiet Sitting Meditation

Quiet sitting meditation may be practiced for fifteen minutes in the beginning and gradually prolonged. In meditation one gathers energy and obtains deep rest; the mind is able to quiet itself as all aspect of one's being connects harmoniously with the universal energies. In this way one experiences and perceives subtle states of consciousness. Meditation allows negativity to surface and be dissolved. It also creates the space for intuitive, creative and inspirational insights.

4. Moving Meditation

Moving meditation is an essential aspect of self-cultivation. Such movement includes various exercises which develop the ability to guide one's internal and external energies. It is characterized by the "Eight Treasures" and "Tai Chi movement." The Eight Treasures are a combination of breathing and energy guidance techniques which open the major channels of the body and allow the gathering of one's own energy and of the subtle energy in one's environment[5]. They may be practiced independently or as a foundation for Tai Chi movement. Tai Chi movement induces the gathering, refinement and circulation of one's energy into more subtle channels. Such moving meditation integrates the body, mind and spirit, harmonizes one's internal energy with the universal law, and leads one to true health. It may be practiced by people of all ages.

5. Invocations

Invocations are a technique for the guidance of subtle energy. They cause the response of the universal law. Through the practice of invocations, one may experientially prove the existence of the spiritual realms for oneself. Practiced diligently and consistently, they will restore one's mind and spirit to their original state of integrity and facilitate the ultimate realization of oneness with Tao[5].

6. Avoid Excessive Sexual Activity

An important part of the Integral Way of Life is the avoidance of excessive sexual activity. Achieved ones are not opposed to sexuality, but they are aware of possible negative influences of sexual activity. Excessiveness in sexual intercourse depletes one's vital energy and causes mental scatteredness and inefficiency. In determining the frequency of sexual activity, one needs to consider the natural rhythm of one's age and physical condition. According to the ancient energy calendar, there are certain days on which sexual intercourse violates the subtle energy of that particular time and may cause physical and mental disturbances. These specific days can be referred to on the ancient developed calendar. Dual cultivation also includes techniques which are taught by an achieved one at the appropriate time and on the appropriate level.

7. Abstain from Certain Foods & Substances

When practicing the Integral Way, one abstains from certain foods and substances such as raw or half-cooked meat, caffeine, strong spices, nicotine, narcotics and recreational drugs, prescription drugs, chemical food additives, improper herbs like peyote, etc., and strong alcoholic beverages.

8. Abstain from Unnecessary Activity

The last basic aspect of disciplining oneself to one's benefit is to abstain from unnecessary activities. Contemporary life is hectic. People spend much time and money in the pursuit of unnecessary "busy-ness." This is an unwise investment of one's life and energy. Eliminating activities which are not essential to one's life and well being allows more time for self-cultivation, quiet reflection or service to a worthwhile cause.

These eight aspects of integral truth are only the fundamental criteria of a healthy and balanced Way of life. If one is sincerely dedicated to one's personal development and spiritual evolution, it is best to seek the guidance and instruction of a true Master.

The Integral Way stresses not doing anything recklessly. One follows the natural Way and avoids violating the natural energy order. Universal law is not created by man but is naturally so. For example, every part of the human body has its own position and function. The vast universe also has an effective natural energy order just like the human body, and it will cause trouble if it is violated. The Integral Way is based on the plain reality of the universe and follows the direct way to restore a human's true formless nature. Its teachings are concise and precise and cultivate the spirit itself.

Spiritual cultivation is composed of one's daily life activities, such as the way of speaking, the way of behaving, and all daily life movements. All of these are important elements of spiritual power development. They are the most elementary spiritual ceremonies. They restore spontaneity and deny any kind of mental manipulation. A natural human being is directed by his spiritual energy and causes appropriate responses not by need, but by pure spontaneity. Without design, one practices the very nature of the universe and connects oneself with universal simplicity. By simplifying one's activities, emotions, mind and spirit, one becomes united with the very essence of the universe. One conducts oneself exactly as a natural being. Then the universe responds not to one's manipulative mind, but to his or her pure spirit. When a human knows and embodies goodness, he or she receives good and beautiful responses. Through strict traditional spiritual training, one may become a completely developed human being.

You can achieve yourself in everyday life by simply accomplishing what needs to be done physically, mentally and spiritually. Spiritual achievement does not come from sitting around waiting for the future to bring you a reward. People establish and follow religions without ever establishing a natural life. No religion can establish natural life. People can only live it.

11 Advice for Advanced Practice

Deepening Your Practice

Practically speaking, the dissolution of the personal self requires devotion. When you begin to learn the form, you must do it correctly. Once you know the form, you can go much deeper with your practice.

The external form is the first level to achieve. To reach true mastery, you must continue to practice until it is not you doing the movement. Then, you continue to practice the movement until your entire life and everything you do merge with the cosmic law and there is no personal self. It takes many years to reach this level, but it is well worth the effort. From the relative movement of yin and yang, the polarized energies, you find the absolute.

The art of gentle movement is very personal, and some people never let others observe them doing it, because it is their personal treasure. A few share it with others.

At the same time that you learn the practice, it is important to understand spiritual self-cultivation, to study general energy channels from acupuncture books, and so forth[1] (see Chapter 8). You do not necessarily need to become an expert, but all the knowledge you obtain supports your learning. It is important to not stay on the surface but go deeper, beyond the movement and the physics. If you learn this, you will experience gentle movement as a kind of self-discovery and discovery of nature. If you practice it regularly, you will achieve many things that cannot be described in words.

Tai Chi and Other Kinds of Exercise

Tight muscles will affect your Tai Chi practice negatively, because they block the flow of qi so that it cannot move smoothly from the tan tien to the limbs. Too much muscle tissue also creates pressure on the internal organs, which is not beneficial. Big muscles look strong, but they do not do much for your actual health.

There are two kinds of exercise. Jogging, tennis, going to the gym and other similar sports mostly build muscles, but do you ever wish your body and mind could meet each other? You are always looking for new friends, but do you ever make friends with your own body? You can also benefit from making friends with your inner being. People generally do not do this, because the eye is built for looking outside. In fact, all the sense organs are made to gather external information, and they eventually cause you to lose contact with your own life. Tai Chi movement, if Tai Chi is a movement, is a basic practice to help you find or reconnect with your own life. It is helpful because it is practical and not hard to learn. It also improves your health and helps break up emotional obstructions. By practicing it, you can learn what energy or qi is. Any movement that is too strong makes you unable to manage the subtlety, softness and delicacy of an energy field.

Tai Chi, Breathing and Alignment

Coordinate your breath correctly. In yin type movements you should inhale. Yin movements are the movements of softening, emptying, gathering, converging, rising and moving upward, withdrawing, bending, surprising, swallowing, lightness, quietness, carving and inward moving. In yang type movements you should exhale. Yang movements are the movements of hardening, solidifying, initiating, opening, descending, forward moving, upward moving, extending, falling, sinking, straightening, expanding, out-sending and out-moving.

Your breathing will naturally become coordinated after many years of practice. If you give too much attention to your breath, you will only become tense. Naturalness is the principle to use when beginning to learn the movements, and just allow the correct breathing to follow. Otherwise you may find yourself giving up, because it is too difficult to coordinate everything at once. This would be a great loss for you as a potential achieved one.

Keep your body upright and aligned with the North Star, which is the axis of the Earth. This is an important spiritual, mental and physical alignment to maintain for both your health and your soul's development. Actually it is best to maintain this connection throughout your general everyday movements of sitting, standing and moving.

Tai Chi and the Aging Process

Spiritual self-cultivation with Tai Chi generates energy and makes you strong. Not only do you feel good, but you will feel revitalized. Tai Chi movement will slow down the natural aging process that comes from exposing yourself to external difficulties such as the urban environments. Self-cultivation is an art and a science that can make your life endlessly enjoyable.

Generally achieved Tai Chi practitioners can slow down the aging process by around ten years, compared to the average person who doesn't practice. Practitioners with better than general skills can slow down the aging process by around 20 years, compared to people of average health. And practitioners with outstanding achievement can slow down the aging process by around 30 to 40 years. Actually, most forerunners of Tai Chi learned to forget their age, but this can be inconvenient in modern times, since personal information is usually needed for verification and identification.

Switch Sides Practice

We are all born with a natural tendency to be either right-handed or left-handed. The habit of using one side of the body too much in daily activities, while the other side does nothing, creates or aggravates an imbalance. In order to correct such imbalanced development, qi practice offers an opportunity to use both sides of the body.

For example, I (OmNi) am right-handed. When I was small, I could not successfully use my left hand to cut the fingernails of my right hand with scissors. My mother suggested that I overcome this shortcoming, so on many occasions, I switched hands when doing things. I learned Tai Chi movement on the right side, as everybody does, but in my personal practice, I reverse the movements and do it also on the left. I usually practice the left more than the right, because I already use my right limbs a lot in daily life. Reversing the right movements and doing them on the left side is not all that difficult to do. Generally, people have more strength on one side than on the other. That seems to be a natural arrangement that cannot be considered a problem. However, I do it just to give myself a small challenge and because I do not wish my left side to become too clumsy.

A Different Way to Organize Your Practice

When I (OmNi) have time, I do the art starting with the left side on odd days and the right side on even days. Or, I do the left ones in the morning and the right ones in the afternoon, or vice versa. If I have a whole hour for practice, first I do Gentle Path because it is slow, then I do Sky Journey because it picks up the energy and is faster. I then finish with Infinite Expansion as a peak to generate internal and external energy. It takes almost 40 minutes for me to do all three. Afterward, I slow down to collect my energy back to normalcy.

This arrangement is only one suggestion or possibility. Practicing the physical arts should always be done flexibly and should never push you. It needs to be adjusted to suit your daily activities and stage of life.

Evolving to Self-Guidance

Tai Chi exercise, as we teach it, has a pure spiritual purpose: for maintaining internal and external unity. Even after years and years of practice, you will never become tired of it. Although we do different forms, they are all the great companions of our lives. Some are suitable to do in certain types of weather, different seasons, days, and hours. When you become achieved, you will know what movements are most suitable for certain times and conditions.

All internal movement is adjustable, depending on your knowledge about yourself. You are not fixed by the form. From reading and from your own achieved spiritual knowledge, you can learn to guide yourself for maximum benefit. Eventually, self-guidance becomes necessary for all who use physical movement to achieve spiritual development.

Special Enjoyment

When we have a chance, we sometimes practice physical arts with harmonious music in a beautiful garden with a sweet breeze and the chirping of birds. The trophy we win is filling our lives with pleasure and joy.

Go Deeper Than the Form

In the beginning, whether you choose Tai Chi movement or Qigong, you must learn the external form, but the form does not necessarily stay the same for the rest of your life. As you progress, you move to another, higher level. The purpose of doing the exercise is not merely to be able to do the form. Ordinary people are always looking for external things to imitate and learn, and then they insist that a form needs to be done a certain way. However, the purpose of Tai Chi movement is to attain something that is not formed. Nevertheless, you have to start with the form. Without a form, we would not have a way to teach you. For example, we teach the Integral Truth. The Integral Truth is not limited to verbal communication. Verbal communication can only convey intellectual achievement, but by means of certain forms, we can teach the Integral Truth by being it and doing it, thus enabling you to see and learn that which underlies the movements. Our wish is that through movements that involve your personal activity, you will come to understand and appreciate the Integral Truth.

Often people ask me (OmNi), "What is the Way?" I have attempted to answer this question at different times, but my words are an intellectual message. That is the nature of words. On the other hand, if people just see or follow me when I am doing Tai Chi movement, even though they are not achieved themselves, they cannot help but notice that all the great principles of spiritual reality are being expressed and manifested. They may not know those principles intellectually, but they get a sense of them from watching the movement. People who go further and learn or master the movement themselves can have a direct experience of this.

Again, people often ask, "What is spiritual teaching?" It is the nature of the universe, and again we use Tai Chi movement to answer them. In the moments when you practice gentle movement, you can find eternity in a flash. When you embrace all of nature, each moment, each movement and each inch of progression all hold the joy of timelessness and eternal youthfulness.

When I (OmNi) was young, I taught literature in a Catholic college. The priests were unhappy with me, because when people came to celebrate mass, which is a Catholic ritual, they saw me doing Tai Chi outside. When they complained I told them, "Can't you see that I am praying too? You just do not understand my prayer." "You should worship God in a godly way," they argued. "The Bible never said that God does Tai Chi Chuan." "If God does not move, there can be no universe," was what I told them. I define Tai Chi as the best interpretation of Genesis.

Tai Chi Practice and Reading

In general, when you lay the foundation for your achievement, you will find that the easiest way to nurture the subtle energy is to practice gentle movement (like Tai Chi) in a quiet place with no one else around. The other thing that is helpful is to always come back to read the *I Ching* and the *Tao Te Ching* to correct your Tai Chi movement. Your deeper and deeper understanding of those works will make your Tai Chi movement more effective. It will also help you attain general health and even go as high as to help you attain your spiritual immortality.

Philosophy helps us understand better, but to realize the goal, gentle movement is a useful tool. It can help us reach our goal of spiritual immortality or at least attain fitness, the health of the three spheres[2] and the spiritual integration of the existing well-being of our personal lives.

The *Tao Te Ching* came not only from Lao Tzu's understanding of universal law, but also from his long study of the *Book of Changes*. Ancient versions of the *Book of Changes* were different from the one we have today. Two versions, with different explanations of the hexagrams, were used for many generations before the version we have today. The version of the *I Ching* that is now in use dates from the beginning of the Chou Dynasty (1122-256 B.C.) and has been in use for over 3,200 years. Despite the external differences of these two versions, the fundamental principle of change or movement has not changed. How was this teaching passed down from so long ago? It was simple: a set of symbols were developed and physical movement was used to teach the spiritual meaning contained in the hexagrams Chyan and K'un. Just like written symbols, gentle movement like Tai Chi or Qi Gong is a natural way to demonstrate the truth of life. Movement is easy to understand and perform without intellectual training.

Tai Chi movement is based on the principle of harmony between yin and yang – two opposing forces. It is the main theme of the *I Ching* or *The Book of Changes and the Unchanging Truth*. Gentleness in movement and life is based on the elucidation of Lao Tzu's written work, the *Tao Te Ching*. As you deepen your study of the *I Ching* and continue to study the *Tao Te Ching*, you can use the principles that you learn in your practice of Tai Chi movement or other energy exercises.

When a student learns the form of Tai Chi Chuan from a teacher and only does that much, his or her achievement will be limited to that much. If he studies the *I Ching*, the *Tao Te Ching*, and all of our books on self-cultivation, he or she can put that understanding into their Tai Chi practice. For example, if you go to school, you learn many things that are not necessarily useful in your life, except perhaps how to make money. Yet once you learn the Way or study the *I Ching* and *Tao Te Ching* deeply enough, everything you have learned will express itself in your Tai Chi practice. It is wonderful; the realization of truth, balance, symmetry, internal and external harmony, and neutrality can all be seen in your Tai Chi practice.

Deeper understanding can be achieved by selective reading. When you read the *Tao Te Ching* and the *I Ching*, your understanding will grow and you will know how to correct your movements. It is not usually a matter of form, but of principle.

You might take a half a year to read one book like the *Tao Te Ching*, but after that half year, your movement will be different and better. If you continue to read good spiritual books, you can eventually express everything you learn from them in your Tai Chi practice. It all depends upon how you go into it.

If you learn Tai Chi, you should confirm your practice with the principles taught in the *Tao Te Ching*. If you have not yet read the *Tao Te Ching*, please read it. It will help you do Tai Chi correctly because of its emphasis on softness over strength. It discourages people from looking for fights, although you can still apply your training in an emergency for self-defense.

You need to have a spiritual goal when you do Tai Chi. If you do well in practicing Tai Chi, you can attain the subtle truth and know that it exists by your own development.

The Importance of Self-Control and Qi in the Spiritual Process

One of the aspects of your being that you must control in pursuing Tai Chi for spiritual development is your mind. The mind usually means one's emotions or psychology as affected by one's living conditions, environment and each individual's sexual energy. You may not yet know that, but all of these – emotions, psychology, living conditions, environment and energy – are controlled by the mind or left to run rampant if there is no self-respect or discipline. Close self-observation will show this to be true.

If a person learns how to control his mind, he can build up his sexual energy (jing). So the next step is to refine the sexual energy to be qi. Now we need to give you a secret. We would like to tell you how to do it. Let us begin by first going deeper.

Qi has multiple functions. One apparent, easily seen function is immunity. For example, if a person has strong qi, it means that the person does not easily become sick. In general, when people catch a cold, it is because a person's immune system is low; thus, he can easily be attacked by a virus. On the other hand, if the person's immunity is strong, then even if there is a flu going around, he will not catch it. This is one function of qi.

However, colds are caught for different reasons. If a person has sudden changes in hot and cold, it can be reason to catch a cold, but that is not related to qi, that is different. We are talking about the immune energy that is called "wei qi." A person's wei qi will be low, for example, if he allows himself to be very tired over a long period of time. Low wei qi is usually caused by poor living habits.

A person who does Tai Chi or internal energy movement is able to transfer his sexual energy into wei qi to enhance his or her immune system. This is why practitioners of Tai Chi do not easily get a cold; their qi flows smoothly throughout the whole body. And this is an interesting thing. If a person who has been practicing Gentle Movement for an extended period of time has sex, he might easily catch a cold the next day. Why? Because qi is something so subtle. It moves between the skin and muscle and can protect a person, but having sex can break the strength of the protection. It can take the qi away from protecting the person, kind of like a leak or damage caused. People who do not do Tai Chi (or Qigong) and have sex are not sensitive to this. They may not catch colds, but they will become run down physically over an extended period of time. It is not that doing Tai Chi will make you catch colds. It is only the sudden change of direction of the qi that caused the problem for the Tai Chi practitioner.

In our tradition, there is some important guidance that we will tell you. First we would like to explain a few things. When you practice Gentle Movement such as Tai Chi or Qigong, you unconsciously increase qi. However, you may not know about it or notice it until you have sex and catch a cold. You think to yourself, why did I get a cold? The answer is that the qi was lost in sexual activity. A Tai Chi practitioner can experience this. An ordinary person has no way to tell how he got a cold, but the Tai Chi practitioner will know that he got a cold from sex.

In ancient times, a teacher of Tai Chi Chuan or other qi exercise would also instruct his students in push hands. Push hands is dual Tai Chi practice. When a person does push hands, the most important thing is his concentration. If you match up two people of equal skill, the one who does not do as well is the one who had sex the night before. His concentration is not as good because the energy was pulled away from his brain. If you learn push hands, you can test this and learn for yourself that sexual activity drains the qi.

We are leading up to telling you the valuable guidance of the ancestors. Their advice was not to be celibate and hide from the opposite sex by living in a cave. Many people who cultivated themselves then, just as now, were married people and had obligations. However, if they wished to have sexual activity, three days beforehand they would stop their practice and become an ordinary person. Then, after sex, they would wait for four days before resuming their Tai Chi Chuan or Qigong practice to restore the normalcy of their energy flow. This is called "chien sang houz" – three days before, four days after. We are glad to have the opportunity to explain this principle to you and to all people so that they can understand and better control their paired or single life situation, rather than going to live in caves.

When a person knows that he would like to maintain a high level of qi rather than have sex, he has broken through one of the great mental obstructions to realizing the Integral Truth. It is passing through a great checkpoint. When a person practices Tai Chi or Qigong and sees the potential or opportunity for personal achievement, and knows that it is better than anything else, he finally learns to stop strong sexual desire. Once you refine that kind of desire, then you can easily break through that obstruction.

People without interest in spiritual life will experience that their Tai Chi or Qigong practice enhances and enforces their sexual capacity. There are descriptions of sexual fantasy that many people can only think about, but people who practice internal energy exercises such as Tai Chi or Qigong can actually fulfill them. Their practice will give them a special capability. A rarely achieved master, doing sexual meditation with the right partner, can last seven days continually without an ejaculation and still be strong. My personal experience is that a person's sexual energy is much increased by Tai Chi or Qigong practice. However, many excellent Tai Chi champions or teachers died young by transferring that power into the fulfillment of sexual fantasies. I do not recommend sexual fantasy as a pursuit, only as a test for your own proof that it is true. If you test it and find that you have that capability, it means that your control over your nervous system is much stronger than that of most people.

In achieving spiritual immortality, most people recognize, as I (OmNi) also did through my personal experience, that refining sexual energy into qi is the second step.

Tai Chi and Your Shen (Spirit)

In your practice, your Shen (the spiritual awareness within your consciousness without any specific content and/or intention) and qi (the subtle, vital force of life before it takes form and becomes jin) should flow smoothly through the changing procession of different postures. Nothing should stick out or be cut off. At all times, move from the deep Shen and qi level of your being to the outer level of your physical being. In other words, Tai Chi practice is about allowing the deep conscious energy to express itself through your body, rather than allowing the specific posture or bodily form to command your body's qi. You can then find the harmony that exists within the variety, and the distinct variety that exists within the unity. As you continue your practice, you will also find that there are more hidden degrees of change relating to the empty force and solid force.

You need to move calmly in order for the Shen to move the qi. This is how you gather chi into your bones. When the qi moves your body, your movements can progress smoothly. The jin (which is refined inner strength that comes from the concentration of qi, rather than from physical muscular force) looks loose but it is not loose; it looks like it is going to spread, but it does not spread; it is in control. When the jin can involve pauses, the qi should flow continuously like an uninterrupted sweet melody.

Attend to your conscious mind and then your body. By keeping your belly free of tension, the qi can gently gather and stretch to enter your spine.

Your consciousness should be comfortable and your body quiet. Always be aware that it is the Shen that you are strengthening.

Once you start to move, remember that as one part of your being moves, all parts of your being follow in exactly the same way, and as one part starts to quiet down, all other parts of your being should quiet down.

Internalizing Tai Chi

Tai Chi is also a principle, so there are different movements and different practices. You can do Tai Chi standing, sitting or lying down. You can also visualize yourself doing it. In the morning, I (OmNi) do a sitting type of Tai Chi called Dao-In. There are different types of Tai Chi movements that are used according to the situation.

We usually talk about internal Tai Chi as being more important than external Tai Chi. The goal is obviously the same, to attain harmony and balance. Without practicing internal Tai Chi, external Tai Chi only reminds your mind to attune yourself. Internal Tai Chi is a system that goes beneath or beyond external form. That is the key.

So, do we do anything besides Tai Chi? Yes, we do lots of things. There is an abundance of ancient methods that were developed through thousands of years of human experience. Few people have the time to learn them all, but at least you know Tai Chi.

Many people think, "I like living in this body, but I would also like to prove that my life extends beyond this physical life." You can use Tai Chi movement to prove this for yourself. I (OmNi) do that practice also: at the beginning I do it intentionally with my mind. When I am asleep, my soul can stand up, walk outdoors and practice Tai Chi from beginning to end and then come back. Usually, if you do one or two movements, you lose yourself and are already asleep again. It is quite difficult to do the whole sequence through, but it is worth a try. It must happen in real sleep. If you use the mind, you will suddenly wake up, because the mind and the soul are different.

Once you have enough training and have practiced persistently, any movement you make can connect your body, mind and spirit. Even if you only think the words, "Tai Chi," you will immediately align yourself in one piece. How do you do it? By deep practice. There is a Chinese proverb that says, "When you learn to do movement, keep doing movement at all times. When you learn to sing, keep singing until you sing well." This means, when you learn Tai Chi movement, move your body as if you were doing Tai Chi movement at all times. This is how you achieve yourself.

There are many spiritual treasures to be learned. Don't feel disappointed if you do not have enough time to learn them all. We are fortunate enough to learn Tai Chi. Tai Chi opens the door to high achievement, and I hope all of you will have the chance to learn it.

When I (OmNi) was young, I traveled to the high mountains to visit many masters. I will tell you the truth: many of them did not know Tai Chi at all! Then how did they live so long and achieve so highly? Each of them knew some simple movement that had a specific benefit. You have already learned much more than any master, but you must practice it. Constancy and persistence are the keys to success. You will learn many things as you continue to practice qi movement and implement the tai chi principle in your everyday life.

Supplementary Cultivation

You may choose a standing cultivation practice for self-healing and self-strengthening. It can become a part of your Tai Chi practice. Standing practices benefit your spine and nervous system, among other things. When your head, shoulders, breathing, mind, eyes and inner qi are poised, vital qi will grow naturally. You can begin with five minutes of quiet standing and gradually increase it to one or several hours. Practice in a quiet, clean and fresh location. The practice can transform your mental rubbish into vitality and, over time, strengthen your immune system in order to fight off chronic disease and pathogens arising from weather and seasonal changes. Such benefits come through perseverance and regular practice.

If you prefer to do sitting meditation, the principle, requirements and effectiveness are the same as the standing practice.

Walking meditation can also be very useful. Personally, I gain a great deal from this practice. Most of my writing visions come about when I practice walking meditation in a natural and fresh environment, such as by the sea, in the mountains, fields, and gardens and along country trails.

Sleeping cultivation is also helpful. Be sure that you sleep on your side, and face towards your personal favorite direction based on the five element system in order to remain balanced.

12 Four Tai Chi Chuan Classics

A Discussion of the Practice of Tai Chi Chuan
(a.k.a., The Theory of Tai Chi Chuan)

The following is adapted from A Discussion of the Practice of Tai Chi Chuan, a traditional text, which is sometimes attributed to Master Zhang San-Feng who lived in the 13th century.

1. When one begins to move, the entire body should be light and flexible, and the movement must be continuous.

2. The qi should be expanded with vitality and the mind tranquil.

3. Do not allow gaps, unevenness or discontinuities.

4. Your feet are the root of energy, which passes through the legs, is controlled by the waist, and finally emerges through the fingers. Your feet, legs and waist need to be coordinated so that in moving forward and backward you have good control of time and space.

5. Without this control of time and space in all movements – up, down, left, right, forward and backward – your body will be in disorder and the fault must be sought in the waist and legs.

6. All these principles concern the will rather than merely the external.

7. When there is up, there must be down; when there is left, there must be right. The will to go up implies the will to go down. For if upon lifting an opposing force you add the idea of pushing it down, then the root of your opposition is broken and without doubt you will overcome it quickly.

8. The empty and solid can be clearly distinguished. Each physical situation by nature has an empty side and a solid side. This is true of every physical situation.

9. Let there be continuity in the movements of the entire body. Let there be not the slightest break.

The Treatise on Tai Chi Chuan

The following is adapted from a work of the same name attributed to Wang Chung-Yueh, the foremost pupil of Zhang San-Feng.

1. Tai Chi, the ultimate form, arises out of wu chi, the Undivided Oneness. It is the origin of movement and stillness, and the Mother of yin and yang. In movement it generates, in stillness it returns.

2. Neither exceeding nor falling short, Tai Chi moves in bending and stretching.

3. When one yields to a hard force, this is called "moving around it." When one tackles with a hard force, this is called 'sticking with it.'

4. When the other's movement comes quickly, respond quickly. When the other's movement comes slowly, follow slowly. In myriad changing situations, the principle is the same.

5. From familiarity with the exercise comes a gradual realization and understanding of energy. From the understanding of energy there comes spiritual illumination. Yet only after long, diligent practice will this sudden seeing through be achieved.

6. Empty and alert, still and quiet. The breath sinks into the lower tan tien.

7. Not inclined, not leaning. Suddenly concealing, suddenly manifesting. When an intruding weight comes to my left, my left is empty. When an intruding weight comes to my right, then my right disappears. Looking up, the other feels my height. Looking down, the other feels my depth. Advancing, he feels the distance lengthening. Retreating, he is more crowded. A small bird cannot take off, because there is no solid part to ascend from. Nor can a single fly land.

8. The opponent does not know where the energy is changing in me, but I alone know where the opponent's force is located. When great heroes are without match, it is because of all of these factors.

9. There are many other techniques of combat. Whatever their differences, they all nevertheless rely on the strong to overcome the weak, and the slow to give in to the fast. Yet as far as the strong beating the weak, the slow giving in to the fast, such things derive from natural abilities and do not have to be studied.

10. When 'four ounces move a thousand pounds' it is obviously not a matter of strength. When an old man can withstand many young men, how can it be through accomplishment of speed?

11. Stand as a poised scale. In action be as a wheel.

12. With the center of your gravity displaced to one side, you can be fluid. If you are 'double heavy,' with your weight evenly distributed on both feet, you become stagnant.

13. Often one encounters someone who even after many years of study has not achieved proper development and is still subdued by others. This is because he has not realized the fault of 'double heaviness.'

14. To avoid this fault, one must know yin and yang. To stick is also to move away and to move away is also to stick. Yin does not leave yang and yang does not leave yin. Yin and yang always complement each other. To understand this is necessary in order to understand energy.

15. When one understands energy, the more one practices, the more wonderful will be his development. One comprehends in silence and experiences in feeling, until gradually one may act at will.

16. There is the traditional advice to deny self and to yield to the other, but many have misunderstood this to mean to abandon the near and to seek the far. Only a true Master has the skill to demonstrate this principle. A mistake of inches but an error of a thousand leagues. Therefore, the student needs to pay careful heed to what is said.

An Internal Explanation of the Practice of the Thirteen Postures

The following is adapted from a work of the same name by Wu Yu-Xiang.

1. The mind moves the qi calmly and naturally, directing it deeply inward; then it can be gathered into the bones and marrow.

2. The qi moves the entire being smoothly and continuously; then the form can easily follow the mind.

3. If your energies are vitalized, then there is no problem about being sluggish and heavy. To accomplish this, the spine needs to be erect as if the head were suspended.

4. The mind and qi must move flexibly in order to achieve smoothness and roundness of movement. This is accomplished by the interchange of yin and yang.

5. To concentrate the energy one must sink one's center of gravity, maintain looseness and quietude, and focus one's energy in a single direction.

6. To stand one must remain centrally poised, calm and expanded, and one can thus protect himself from all sides.

7. Move the energy like a delicate string of pearls so there is no place that the energy does not reach. Refine your essence to become like flawless steel so there is no obstruction it cannot destroy.

8. The appearance is as a hawk catching a rabbit; the spirit, as a cat watching a mouse.

9. In resting be as still as a mountain; in movement be like a river.

10. Store the energy as if drawing a bow. Issue the energy as if releasing the arrow. Through the curve seek the straight. First store then release.

11. The energy issues from the spine. Steps follow changes in the form.

12. To withdraw is to release. To release is to withdraw. To break is to continue.

13. Back and forth must have folds, no straight path in either case, in order to prepare and gather the energy. Advancing and retreating must have turns and changes.

14. Through what is greatly soft one achieves what is greatly strong.

15. If one is able to inhale and exhale, then one can be light and flexible.

16. Breathing must be nourished without impediment, no holding of the breath and no forcing it, then no harm will come.

17. The energy must be bent like a bow and stored, then you will always have more than you need.

18. The mind orders, the qi goes forth as a banner, the waist takes the command.

19. First seek to stretch and expand; afterwards seek to tighten and collect; then one attains integrated development.

20. It is said: First the mind, afterwards the body. The abdomen is relaxed, the qi is gathered into the bones, the spirit is at ease and the body quiet.

21. At every moment be totally conscious.

Essential Principles for Practicing Tai Chi Chuan

The following is adapted from a work of the same name by W.S. Wu (1812-1880).

1. As one part moves, all parts move; if one part is still, all parts are still.

2. Pull and move, go and come, the qi goes to the back and is gathered in the spine, making the spirit firm and leisurely manifesting calm without.

3. Use force as if pulling silk.

4. Throughout the body concentrate on the spirit and not on the qi.

5. To concentrate on the qi causes stagnancy.

6. To be with qi, or holding the breath, is to be without strength. To be without qi, moving the breath and allowing it to flow freely, one can be really strong.

7. The breath is like a cart's wheel. The waist is like its axle.

PART FOUR:
THE NI FAMILY TAOIST TAI CHI TRADITION

13 The Spiritual Background of the Union of Tao and Man

"In the tenth moon plum-blossoms bloom,

Awaiting the early arrival of the spring.

If inanimate things can predict nature's Way,

It would be folly for us not to follow the Tao."

(Lu Tung-Ping)

The spiritual roots of the "Union of Tao and Man" can be traced back to prehistoric times. The Chinese believe that before Emperor Fu Shi, who is said to have reigned around 8,000 years ago, the Earth was inhabited by gods. These supernatural beings came into existence as the result of the combination of the subtle, creative energy of the universe with the pure, physical energy of the Earth. These gods lived spontaneously and intuitively in perfect harmony with nature and had no need of any method of self-cultivation or restoration. Their lives were manifestations of pure natural law.

The period after Fu Shi until the end of the reign of the great Emperor Yu (2205-2125 B.C.) was known as the age of the semi-gods. During this period, the Emperors were profoundly spiritual and wise people who were deeply involved in researching and practicing esoteric methods which would restore their divine quality. Fu Shi is attributed with the discovery of the eight manifestations of the *I Ching*; the famous Yellow Emperor, Huang Ti (2697-2597 B.C.), was the author of the classic on internal medicine; and the great Emperors Niao (2357-2258 B.C.) and Shun (2255-2208), all practiced and handed down the Taoist Sacred Method until the reign of the son of Emperor Chih (2125-2116 B.C.). The Emperor Chih was the first to inherit the throne through family succession, whereas previously it has been passed only to sages. Those who succeeded Emperor Chih were unable to attain the heavenly qualities of sages, so the age of the semi-gods came to an end.

Then came an era of leaders who were not spiritually developed. In this era, the Taoist Sacred Method was no longer handed down by Emperors but was transmitted generation after generation by inspired sages called shiens who lived in high mountains as hermits, apart from the masses who abused themselves through their life style. These enlightened people lived simply, in harmony with nature, and enjoyed the unceasing regenerative power of the universe. Sometimes shiens would come to live among people, but they generally went unrecognized because they hid their great wisdom and miraculous powers. Sometimes they traveled throughout the countryside helping people in need. Most of them, however, chose to reside quietly in the remote mountains far from the tumult of the world.

To attain Tao

It is not necessary

    to go to the mountains.

Stay right here.

    In the red dust, riding a golden horse –

      there is a great practitioner of Tao.

Thus it is said

    the mountains provide only quietude.

      (Lu, Tung Ping)

Prior to the Han dynasty (206 B.C. – 219 A.D.) the teaching of Tao was a pure spiritual tradition involved with restoring the divine nature of human beings through the cultivation of Tao, and was studied and practiced only by shiens and their disciples in the high mountains. These shiens were the forefathers of my tradition, the "Union of Tao and Man." Close to the end of the Han dynasty (c. 184 A.D.) a local religious cult, "The Yellow Hood" which also called itself Taoism, appeared. Several such cults existed in different ages. However, those religious movements must not be confused with the pure, spiritual tradition of ancient Taoism which I call the Integral Way. They must never be mistaken for the ancient teaching of the high shiens.

What is Tao?

It is just this.

It cannot be rendered into speech.

If you insist on an explanation,

This means exactly this. (Lu, Tung Ping)

One of the most famous shiens at the end of the Han dynasty was Kou Hong (205 A.D.). Inspired by his immortal grand-uncle, he went to Tien Tai Mountain in Chekiang Province to practice the secret formula of sublimation and refinement. He authored the book *Pao Po Tzu*, a collection of all the methods of self-cultivation in existence at that time. The theoretical part of his work has been translated into English. He succeeded in his cultivation and became an Immortal. In the same mountains, but in the Tang dynasty (618-906 A.D.), the Master Sz Ma Chung Jen, the author of *The Theory of Sitting, Forgetting and Uniting*, and his teacher, known as "The Son of Invisible Heaven," who authored a book of this title, both cultivated themselves and practiced the Taoist Sacred Method.

The elixir of immortality:

There is no need to beg from others.

The eight trigrams,

The nine colors

Are all on your palms.

The five elementary formations,

The four figures of the diagrams,

All are within you.

Understanding this

You can communicate with the spirits. (Lu, Tung Ping)

All of the famous "Eight Immortals" are descendants of the sacred tradition of the "Union of Tao and Man." The most famous of them is Master Lu Tung-Ping, who lived during the Tang dynasty and whose poems are quoted herein. The story of Lu Tung-Ping's enlightenment is contained in the famous play of the Yuan dynasty entitled "The Yellow Millet Dream." This play depicts Lu Tung-Ping as a scholar traveling to the capital to take the court examination in hope of becoming appointed to a government position. He stopped one evening at a roadside inn where, while he was waiting for his supper of yellow millet to be cooked, he fell asleep. He dreamt that he went through many distressing circumstances until he finally met Chung-Li Ch'uan, who opened his eyes to the truth. Upon his awakening from the dream, eighty years of life experience had already passed.

Master Lu lived during the period of Chinese history when Buddhism was starting to flourish in China. He departed from the typical monastic custom of avoiding the people of the world and traveled around the country teaching the truth of immortal life.

People may sit until the cushion is worn through,

But never quite know the real Truth;

Let me tell you about the ultimate Tao:

It is here, enshrined within us. (Lu, Tung Ping)

Master Lu's disciple Leao Hai Chan, was the Premier to the Emperor Yen (c. 911 A.D.). Leao Hai Chan passed the Sacred Method to Shueh Bau Guan, who passed it to Shih Sing Ling, who passed it to Bai Yu Chan. These five shiens are called the "Five Forefathers of the Southern Branch."

Close your eyes to seek the Truth

And Truth comes naturally.

The pearl of Tao emits liveliness.

Play with it day and night,

And never throw it away

Lest the God of the Netherworld

Send his underlings after you. (Lu, Tung Ping)

I (OmNi) myself am a descendant of the shiens of Tien Tai Mountain, where Kou Hung refined his elixer of immortality. The Taoist temple in Tien Tai Mountain was built in memory of the enlightenment of the Taoist Prince Tung Pa, the son of the Emperor Ling Wang (571-543 B.C.) of the Chou dynasty. Master Sz Ma Chung Jen of the Tang dynasty (618-906 A.D.) is the remote spiritual heir of Master Dao Hong-Cheng of the Chen dynasty (265-588 A.D.). Both, he and master Jang Tse Yang of the Sung dynasty (960-1276 A.D.) cultivated in Tien Tai Mountain, and were part of the Southern Branch.

The Northern, Western and Eastern Branches were all formed separately. The Northern Branch started during the Yuan dynasty (1277-1367 A.D.) with Wang Jung Yang, who tried to preserve the Chinese from destruction by the invading Mongols. The most striking difference between this branch and the others is their strict practice of independent cultivation with celibacy for the novice. The Western and Eastern Branches were formed during the Ming dynasty (1368-1644 A.D.) and Ching dynasty (1644-1912 A.D.), respectively. Both schools share the same truths, the only difference being in a few secret techniques of cultivation.

Some of the Masters of the sacred family of shiens which constitute my lineage are:

1. Master Shih Ga or "Stone Drum" – his name comes from the practice of engraving mystical pictographs in stone; he lived in the Da Lu Mountains in Shueh-An County of Chekiang Province;

2. Master Shih Je or "Stone Disaster" – his name comes from his liking to break stones with his forehead; he lived in the South Yen Tang Mountains in Ping Yang County of Chekiang Province;

3. Master Tai Huang or "Great Wilderness" – who lived in the Da Lu Mountains;

4. Master Wei Fong or "Revolving Peak" – his name comes from the fact that the wild geese on their journey south or north would circle around the peak of the mountain he lived on in the North Yen Tang Mountains;

5. Master Teah Yuhn or "Crown of Strength" – his name depicts his strong virtues; he lived in the Mao Mountains in Chu Yung County of Kuansu Province;

6. Master Tung Yuhn or "Purple Clouds" – his name comes from the appearance of purple clouds in the sky at the time he achieved enlightenment;

he is Grandmaster Yosan Ni (the father of Hua Ching Ni and grandfather of Mao Shing Ni) and lived in Chekiang Province; he practiced ancient Taoism (the Integral Way) and integral medicine;

7. Master Yen Tang Jung or the "Hermit of Yen Tang;"

8. Master Tai Ruh Yin Yung or the "Hermit of Tai Ruh;"

9. Master Da Tao Tzu or the "Son of the Eternal Tao" – he is the author, Hua-Ching Ni (OmNi).

10. Master Ying Luan or the "Messenger of the Great Mystery" – he is the author, Mao Shing Ni.

> Sojourning in the Ta-Yu Mountains,
>
> Who converses with the white crane
>
> That comes flying?
>
> How many times have the mountain people
>
> Seen the winter plum-flowers blossoming.
>
> Spring comes and goes,
>
> Deep in fallen flowers and streams.
>
> People are not aware
>
> Of the many immortals around them. (Lu, Tung Ping)

In spiritual teaching, more important than anything else is giving authentic teaching based on actual spiritual achievement. Anyone who wants to can trace the lineage of my (OmNi's) tradition. The names of teachers of Sun Ching (Shangqing) School, different sects of the Golden Immortal Medicine School (my father was related to those schools and with our family tradition) and the Jing Ming School (my mother was related to that school) in different generations were recorded in the Taoist Canon, the collection of 1487 spiritual books. Although the Taoist Canon has enormous volumes, it still cannot include all the teachings and all the names of the people in spiritual activity during the last 5,000 years. There are still other collections of scattered Taoist spiritual books, which can serve as a partial reference. This collection was compiled between 1436 and 1446 A.D. during the Ming Dynasty.

ABOUT TAOIST MASTER HUA CHING NI (OmNi)

Master Hua-Ching Ni (OmNi) is fully acknowledged and empowered as a true Master of Tao. He is heir to the wisdom transmitted through an unbroken succession of 74 generations of Taoist Masters dating back to 216 B.C. As a young boy, he was educated within his family and then studied more than 31 years in the high mountains of China, fully achieving all aspects of Taoist science and metaphysics.

In addition, 38 generations of the Ni family have practiced natural Taoist medicine. OmNi has continued this in America with clinics and the establishment of Yo San University of Traditional Chinese Medicine.

As a young boy, OmNi was educated by his family in the spiritual foundation of Tao. Later, he learned Taoist arts from various achieved teachers, some of whom have a long traditional background. OmNi worked as a traditional Chinese doctor and taught Taoist learning on the side as a service to people. He taught first in Taiwan for 27 years by offering many publications in Chinese and then in the United States and other Western countries since 1976. To date, he has published about more than 50 books in English, made four DVDs of Taoist movements and wrote several dozen Taoist songs sung by an American singer.

OmNi stayed about 31 years in the mountains in different stages. He thinks the best way to live, when possible, is to be part-time in seclusion in the mountains and part-time in the city doing work of a different nature. He believes this is better for the nervous system than staying only in one type of environment.

The 50 books that OmNi has written in Chinese include 2 books about Chinese medicine, 5 books about Taoist spiritual cultivation and 4 books about the Chinese internal school of martial arts. The above were published in Taiwan. He has also written two unpublished books on Taoist subjects.

The other unpublished 33 books were written by brush in Chinese calligraphy during the years he attained a certain degree of achievement in his personal spiritual cultivation. OmNi said, "Those books were written when my spiritual energy was rising to my head to answer the deep questions in my mind. In spiritual self-cultivation, only by nurturing your own internal spirit can communication exist between the internal and external spirits. This can be proven by your personal spiritual stature. For example, after nurturing your internal spirit, through your thoughts, you contact many subjects which you could not reach in ordinary daily life. Such spiritual inspiration comes to help when you need it. Writings done in good concentration are almost like meditation and are one fruit of your cultivation. This type of writing is how internal and external spiritual communication can be realized. For the purpose of self-instruction, writing is one important practice of the Jing Ming School or the School of Pure Light. It was beneficial to me as I grew spiritually. I began to write when I was a teenager and my spiritual self awareness had begun to grow."

In his books published in Taiwan, OmNi did not give the details of his spiritual background. It was ancient Taoist custom that all writers, such as Lao Tzu and Chuang Tzu, avoided giving their personal description. Lao Tzu and Chuang Tzu were not even their names. However, OmNi conforms with the modern system of biographies and copyrights to meet the needs of modern society.

OmNi's teaching differs from what is generally called Taoism in modern times. There is no comparison or relationship between his teaching and conventional folk or religious Taoism. OmNi describes his independent teaching as having been trained without the narrow concept of lineage or religious mixture of folk Taoism. It is non-conventional and differs from the teaching of any other teachers.

OmNi shares his own achievement as the teaching of rejuvenated Taoism, which has its origins in the prehistoric stages of human life. OmNi's teaching is the Integral Way or Integral Taoism. It is based on the Three Scriptures of Taoist Mysticism: Lao Tzu's *Tao Te Ching*, *The Teachings of Chuang Tzu* and *The I Ching* (The Book of Changes). OmNi has translated and elucidated these three classics into versions which carry the accuracy of the most valuable ancient message. His other books are materials for different stages of learning Tao. He has also absorbed all the truthful and highest spiritual achievements from various schools to assist the illustration of Tao with his own achieved insight on those different levels of teachings.

The ancient Taoist writing contained in the Three Scriptures of Taoist Mysticism and all Taoist books of many schools were very difficult to understand, even for Chinese scholars. Thus, the real Taoist teaching is not known to most scholars of later generations, the Chinese people or foreign translators. It would have become lost to the world if OmNi, with his spiritual achievement, had not rewritten it and put it into simple language. He has practically revived the ancient teaching to make it useful for all people.

It is the true, traditional spirit of the teaching of Tao, different from some leaders in later times who made it as the mixed Taoist religion. Toward society, the teaching of Tao serves as public spiritual education. Toward individuals, the teaching guides internal spiritual practice. Therefore, the true teaching of Tao has nothing to do with any religions which use formality and damage the true, independent spirit. Although some traditional practice has some external layout, it is the symbol of spiritual practice and some postures which are for guiding or conducting energy in the body. Since its beginnings, this true tradition of Tao has been independent of social limitation. It has also never been involved with the competition of any social religion because this tradition's goal is to help the spiritual development of individuals, broad human society, all religion and culture. Its spiritual teaching is above the confusion of custom and fashionable thought which happens in the frame of time and location. The teaching of Tao serves a deeper and higher sphere of limited life.

Throughout the world, OmNi teaches the simple, pure message of his spiritual ancestors to assist modern people in understanding life and awakening to Tao. Taoist Master Hua-Ching Ni (OmNi) has spoken out and clearly offered more teaching than any other true Taoist master in history. With his achieved insight, over 80 years of training and teaching, and his deep spiritual commitment, OmNi shares his own achievement as the pure, rejuvenated teaching of the Integral Tao.

ABOUT TAOIST MASTER MAO SHING NI

Dr. Mao Shing Ni, Ph.D., D.O.M., L.Ac., ABAAHP or Dr. Mao (as he is known by his patients and students) is a doctor of Chinese medicine and an authority in the field of Taoist anti-aging medicine. He was born into a medical family spanning many generations and started his medical training with his father, a renowned physician of Chinese medicine and Taoist master, and continued his trainings in medical schools in the U.S. and China. After receiving two doctorate degrees and completing his Ph.D. dissertation on Nutrition, Dr. Mao did his postgraduate work at Shanghai Medical University's affiliated hospitals and began his 20-year study of centenarians of China. Dr. Mao returned to Los Angeles in 1985 and has since focused on women's health, immune system related conditions and anti-aging medicine in his practice at the Tao of Wellness in Santa Monica, California with his brother, Dr. Daoshing Ni. Over the years, he has received numerous awards including "Outstanding Acupuncturist of the Year" and "L.A.'s Best".

Dr. Mao is a board-licensed acupuncturist in the state of California and a board certified anti-aging specialist from the American Board of Anti-Aging Health Practitioner. He is a co-founder, past president and current Chancellor of Yo San University of Traditional Chinese Medicine in Los Angeles, where he is active in teaching both students and practitioners. He is also heir to the Integral Way spiritual tradition passed down from his father, having trained in classical Taoist arts and sciences, ranging from Tai Chi, Qi Gong, Taoist yoga, meditation, *I-Ching*, feng shui and face reading. He continues his father's work by writing, lecturing and teaching internationally.

Dr. Mao's published works include the bestselling *Secrets of Longevity, Secrets of Self Healing, Chinese Herbology, Tao of Nutrition, Meditations for Stress Release, Pain Management, Ageless: Smooth Transitions Through Menopause, The Yellow Emperor's Classic of Medicine, The New Universal Morality, Harmony Tai Chi, Energy Enhancement Exercises, Self Healing Qi Gong*, and *The Power of the Feminine*. He was on the editorial board for the best selling book, *Alternative Medicine: the Definitive Guide*. His latest book, *Second Spring: Hundreds of Natural Secrets for Women to Revitalize and Regenerate at Any Age* is published by Simon & Schuster.

Dr. Mao has conducted Tai Chi, Qi Gong meditation and longevity retreats throughout the world. He has lectured internationally on various topics including women's health, menopause, preventive medicine, longevity medicine, diet and nutrition, herbal therapy, stress management, Taoist meditation, lifestyle enhancement, integrative cancer care, Harmony Tai Chi, Self-Healing Qi Gong, Dao-In and spiritual development. Dr. Mao has appeared in numerous interviews on public radio, prime time TV shows and major print media including Dr. Oz, The Doctors, Good Day L.A., Eye on L.A., NBC News, CBS Evening News, Which Way L.A., New York Times, L.A. Times and others. He is a lifetime member of the National Qigong Association.

14 Esoteric Tai Chi Chuan: Ni Family Styles The School of Internal Harmony

Harmony Tai Chi Movement[1]

Purpose: Coordination of the entire body

Center: All three tan tien

Goal: Balancing the energy

There are many styles of Tai Chi being taught in Taiwan and China today. Harmony Tai Chi is similar to those styles, yet it maintains a gracefulness, naturalness and evenness that exceeds any of the newer styles. As its name implies, it brings about unity between the body, mind and spirit. It is a good practice for people of any age for health, enjoyment and artistic intention. It is the most suitable style for people who admire and would like to learn some simple Tai Chi.

In our teaching of the Integral Way, the path of spiritual self-development, the Eight Treasures is required, along with Harmony Tai Chi. Other styles of Tai Chi are not required, because they are for more advanced students who have a higher interest, ambition or enjoyment.

Harmony Tai Chi movement (also called Trinity Style, Unity movement, or Internal Harmony Tai Chi) contains the essence of the Chen, Yang and Wu styles. Chen movement was developed earlier than Yang and Wu, which are later, simplified styles. The Chen Style, which alternates between strength and softness, originally developed from martial arts. The Yang Style tends to be gentle and slow. The Wu style tends to be lighter and faster.

Since Harmony Tai Chi has a balanced focus on integrating the body, mind and spirit, it is the style most suitable for men or women of all ages. Because of its unique quality of capturing the essence of the Yang, Chen and Wu styles of Tai Chi, Harmony Tai Chi saves the serious students of Eastern Health and philosophy the necessity to learn these other styles separately. Instead, it allows for more time to pursue higher forms of learning that are specific in one's cultivation of directing the focus on each of the three tan tiens.

One will readily note the expression of yin and yang energies throughout the Contained (Part I) and Expansive (Part II) segments of the long form, alternating between the two polarities in a continuum. The experience of this graceful dance of yin and yang energies teaches one to become more aware of the Universal Subtle Law in his or her daily life, immediately righting the imbalance and maintaining equilibrium in one's thoughts and action to avoid violating the natural law. Harmony Tai Chi, as its name implies, harmonizes and unifies all three spheres of the human being, allowing its practitioner to experience his or her entire being in synchrony—the Spirit attains clarity in guiding the mind, the Mind achieves impartiality in communicating with the body, the Body carries out its physiology in sustaining life.

Harmony Tai Chi captures the gracefulness and the meditative benefits of the popular Yang Style, the power generating aspects of the Chen Style, and the agility of the Wu Style. It distills the unique benefits of all three styles into one form that can be easily learned by anyone who is interested in improving their health and well-being. Many serious students may learn Trinity Style as a stepping stone to the higher forms of Tai Chi movement such as Gentle Path, Sky Journey or Infinite Expansion.

Harmony Tai Chi is a standing movement, done faster than Qigong with movements that are more sequential than the Eight Treasures. It takes about 5 minutes to perform the beginner's 18-Step Harmony Tai Chi form, 8 minutes to perform the intermediate 28-Step form, and 25 to 30 minutes to perform the advanced 108-Step long form.

Gentle Path Tai Chi Movement[2]

Purpose: Strengthen and refine the hormonal system

Center: Lower tan tien

Goal: Control and refinement of sexual desire

Gentle Path Tai Chi movement focuses on nurturing the lower tan tien, which is the central point between the navel and the sexual organs. This area is connected with the breath. Have you ever observed how you and other people breathe? When a baby breathes, the whole cavity of the baby's trunk, from its shoulders down to its legs, stretches and contracts. The lower tan tien works together with the lungs to allow the baby to breathe fully. However, as most people grow older, their breath becomes shorter and shorter until it can barely fill the lungs any more. That is dangerous, because the lower tan tien is the center of natural vitality in most people. This is especially true of men and physical workers. Although today more people do intellectual work, their vitality still relies on the lower tan tien.

Each movement of Gentle Path Tai Chi tonifies the lower tan tien, which in turn strengthens and enlivens you. Deep, full breathing while doing the exercise is another fortifying factor. All areas in the abdominal cavity produce vital energy that stays in the organs. The lower tan tien is the storehouse of one's physical essence or jing and vitality. This physical vitality consists of kidney essence inherited from one's parentage and nutritional essence from a healthy digestive system. The abundance of this jing essence provides for normal development of the body and brain, structure and function, fertility and creativity. Jing deficiency gives rise to low energy, poor memory, weak bones and muscles, impotence and infertility, hair and teeth loss, and other signs of premature aging. Gentle Path Tai Chi directly affects and benefits the lower tan tien, helping its practitioner restore vitality and essence and thus benefiting the quality and length of one's life.

Sometimes the pattern of these movements is stretching and gathering. When you stretch, your energy moves throughout your whole body. When you contract or gather, the energy returns to the center of your body. It requires time and practice, good control and awareness of your breathing to become effective and precise in coordinating your energy with the movements.

Why is this exercise called Gentle Path? Because it is based on the principles of the *Tao Te Ching*, which teaches us how to be gentle in our lives. It also teaches us to be nonviolent in our emotions, in our personal attitudes and in our physical actions. Many people understand the value of being gentle, but they cannot be that way unless they have achieved internal harmony.

General education uses intellectual knowledge as a tool. People know and tell each other to be gentle, but it is more important to be able to do it in your life. The physical and spiritual education you receive from doing this gentle exercise will help you stay calm in rough situations and handle them gently and smoothly. This is only one of its many benefits.

Gentle Path Tai Chi is sometimes called the Earth Style or Style of Wisdom. Gentle Path is a standing movement, done faster than Qigong with movements that are more sequential than the Eight Treasures. It takes about 40 minutes to perform the entire sequence.

Sky Journey Tai Chi Movement[3]

Purpose:	Uniting with nature
Center:	Middle tan tien
Goal:	Soften the body and increase the qi

Sky Journey's central focus is the middle tan tien, which is located in the thoracic cavity at the point between the nipples (heart area). The middle tan tien is one of the places where you gather energy. Because this exercise was specifically designed and structured to be high, with the center in the middle tan tien, it is not suitable to squat or bend too low while doing it. It should be done with the body gently erect and with the knees straight or only slightly bent.

The middle tan tien is the residence of the Heart or the Mind. Traditional knowledge merges the heart and mind symbolically as one, but physiologically the heart contains up to 60% nerve cells which in turn confirms the heart-mind link. The mind is the instrument of the spirit and when the mind is allowed to rebel, there is discord within one's life. Originally, one comes into this world with a naturally wholesome and impartial mind but with the artificial influence of human society, one's mind becomes corrupted, filled with unnatural thought patterns and abnormal impulses. An unhealthy mind gives rise to emotional problems which can cause strained relationships and lead to paralysis in one's life. Sky Journey Tai Chi works on bringing balance and harmony into the middle tan tien and helps one restore the naturalness and innocence of their mind. It reconnects the mind with that of the heavenly mind.

According to natural cosmology, human beings are the middle point in universal development between the physical world and the spiritual world. Without human life, the energies of Heaven and Earth would separate and have no chance to meet each other. Your life is the bridge between Heaven and Earth.

Most of the movements of this exercise are for the purpose of energy conducting, although they once had a martial purpose. Their purpose now, however, is to defeat certain untamed parts of oneself. Sky Journey is a little faster than other Tai Chi movements such as Gentle Path. It is in the middle range of speed, but it is still not the fastest. If you do it too fast, you will not perform the details correctly, and its effect will be lessened.

Sky Journey is suitable for all people, but it is especially suitable for women, because women generally benefit from maintaining their energy in the middle tan tien. This exercise is also good for men of all ages, because the middle tan tien is a safe spot to pay attention to and cultivate.

All practices have different purposes and goals. Sky Journey, as the middle way, can be a preparation for a further, higher learning. For example, you can use Sky Journey to pacify your emotions, or you can use it to excite and stimulate your body. You can also use it to go in the direction of learning the art of weapons or just do it for self-adjustment and self-control. From a central point, you can go anywhere.

The purpose of practicing the Sky Journey is to learn how to make smooth transitions in life. That is its main benefit, in addition to physical health. Doing this exercise, you can come closer to the Way than by only reading books.

Sky Journey Tai Chi is also referred to as "Mankind Style" or "Style of Harmony with People." It takes approximately 20 minutes to complete Sky Journey Tai Chi Movement.

Infinite Expansion Tai Chi Movement[4]

Purpose: Self-generation of the body

Center: Upper tan tien and central axis

Goal: Self-authority over physical life and spontaneous response to danger

Infinite Expansion was previously called "The Heavenly Ladder," "Uniting with Heaven" or "The Style of Integration," all of which describe the motion of this exercise. When you practice it, you feel as though you are climbing clouds, because frequently you bend and bring your knee close to your abdomen like climbing a ladder. It also feels as though you are a bird in flight. Infinite Expansion is very different from Gentle Path and Sky Journey. It is closer to martial arts and can be excellent training in that regard. Infinite Expansion is thus practiced at a higher range and speed. It focuses on the axis that runs from the top of the head down the middle of the body to the perineum. The top of the head is called "Hundred Meeting" (Du 20 or Baihui), which is the meeting point of yang energy. The trunk of the human body basically has a rounded shape. The center of the body has an axis similar to that of the hub of a wheel, and the spokes all meet at the hub.

The upper tan tien is the connection to the heavenly realm. It is the way station whereby hundreds of spiritual energies within and without one's being gathers. A highly cultivated upper tan tien allows one to possess clarity of vision for one's life and connection to the heavenly realm. When this center is blocked or obscured, one's spirit becomes dull, disturbed or even withered, contributing to a life of emotional turmoil, physical breakdowns and unhappiness. The practice of Infinite Expansion cultivates the upper tan tien, leading to the experience of Infinity.

Infinite Expansion is considered the earliest form of Tai Chi movement and is believed to have been taught by initiated masters and refined through generations before being passed down to us. It was a secret, high achievement in martial arts, taught only to a special few, not to aggressive students. In China, few people have the chance to learn it or understand it. I offer it to all people as an excellent form of physical training. High achievement depends on an individual's devotion.

You can practice Infinite Expansion while listening to good music as a background to help you move and lend recreation to the exercise. You feel great when you do it, as though you are reaching somewhere. Nothing else gives you the same experience with equal benefit. It can prevent you from aging fast, or even make you forget your age altogether. It is light and a delight. If your goal is to go beyond all limitations, you can achieve it through this exercise. However, you need to practice until you perfect it. First develop skill, then go beyond the skill to reach the heights of spiritual bliss.

In spiritual learning, we talk about unlimitedness or the Infinite, but in practical worldly life we need limits. For example, you cannot talk without limits. If you do, people will not trust you any more. You cannot eat without limits. If you do, you will become obese. You cannot drink without limits. In China, the elders of almost every family drink rice wine in the wintertime. Rice wine is not like Japanese sake. Sake is thin and Chinese rice wine is thick. Thick wine is more tonifying and does not cause headaches. Older people usually consider rice wine a tonic, and they do not drink too much. However, if they go past healthy limits and drink unlimitedly, they become drunk.

So, whatever you do, it seems you must have limits. When I say, "no need to have limits," I mean you cannot go beyond what is healthy, useful, truthful, necessary or appropriate. If you do, you will make trouble for yourself. Having limits does not mean that people manage you. You learn to manage and control yourself. When you learn self-control, all your movements are proper and skillful in any situation.

Once you are achieved in Infinite Expansion, you are not limited by your physical body, and you can go beyond this set of movements. Some masters practice it devotedly. It was recorded that one master, in his old age, could do this art in the snow without leaving a trace. That is going beyond physical law. Some masters achieved invisibility. This is also a spiritual practice.

There are three aspects to Infinite Expansion movement. The first is self-control, the second is the whirlpool formation of the energy, and the third is internal energy surfing. An untrained eye might not be able to see those subtleties, so I am explaining them to you. I hope that once you understand these points, you will be inspired to practice.

Infinite Expansion has another interesting aspect, which is the tradition of spiritual swordsmanship. That tradition has an invocation that is used as a spiritual practice. I was told that if you practice that invocation, you will receive energy from nature. Generally, the art of movement is enough and complete in itself.

The practice of Infinite Expansion is suitable for anyone who has learned other Tai Chi movements. The specific value of Infinite Expansion is its circular or cyclical movements. All movements that appear to move outward actually follow a spiral or going out and then retreating.

I (OmNi) have practiced Infinite Expansion more than the other styles, because it is so convenient. It can be done in a big or a small space. A space as small as the top of a dining table is big enough.

In ancient times, it was not allowed to show Infinite Expansion movement to others. Anyone who saw it might think it was a martial art and would challenge the peace-seeking practitioner to a fight, so he usually stayed indoors to avoid trouble. Of course, if you practice indoors, you should open a window to let in fresh air. In modern times, it is okay to do it outdoors, because now people will usually not challenge you.

The flow of energy in Infinite Expansion is like the ocean; you can go everywhere, endlessly. You go beyond, and nothing can restrain you. Have you experienced the infinite? Infinity can be experienced in movement or in quietude. What does infinity mean? Dear friends, you must find out for yourselves. To do so is a challenge and a training. From your practice, you may reach Infinity.

It takes about 20 minutes to perform Infinite Expansion on both the left and right sides.

Sword Practice

Purpose: Spiritual concentration

Center: Upper tan tien

Goal: Spiritual enhancement

At one stage of my (OmNi) life I liked all sword practice because it is much more graceful than general martial arts. I limit it to being my personal enjoyment as a form of spiritual cultivation on a level that transforms the spirit from my hormonal level to become qi and transfers the general physical qi to become Shen, spiritual potency. With this in mind, I think that sword practice can be considered a spiritual practice.

As we view it, general sword dancing is for pleasure and has no spiritual meaning, although it has a lot of graceful postures and movements. It is great to watch women, children, or old people do a sword dance. If you use sword practice for spiritual purposes, however, then it will help your cultivation.

Qigong, Dao-In and Eight Treasures can be the foundation on which practices such as martial arts, sword practice and push hands can be based.

In our school, the School of Internal Harmony, the sword is not used for fighting or fencing. It is for developing spiritual concentration. Having good spiritual concentration affects the health of your body, mind and spirit in a positive way.

OmNi's Experience: The Movements Have Practical Value

I (OmNi) learned several styles of gentle movement from my father's teachers and those who learned with him. Most people know one style but never learn a second. I learned all the essential arts of the internal school, four Tai Chi movements, Cosmic Tour Ba Gua, and Dao-In, because my father's teachers and friends were kind to me. They knew that times were radically changing in China and if these arts were not taught, they would be lost.

First I learned Dao-In, Eight Treasures and Harmony Tai Chi movement. As a boy, I was particularly attentive to those practices because I was not naturally endowed with great physical ability. Then, in order to develop stronger qi, I started to do the penguin-type walk of Cosmic Tour Ba Gua to strengthen my legs. I did it swiftly in the forest to see if I could keep my center of gravity low and still avoid hitting the trees. That training helped me become more agile, but I was unable to manage my movements in an ideal condition. Then I learned Gentle Path Tai Chi Movement, which gently builds one's energy.

After practicing Gentle Path for some time, I felt that I needed to lighten and lift my energy from the lower part of my body, so I learned Sky Journey Tai Chi and Infinite Expansion Tai Chi, which are close to martial arts. In doing them, a person does not fight with anyone, but attains proficiency in movement. Essentially, you learn good control of your body's movements. Good movement brings poise and places a person in an undefeatable position in the first place.

Different kinds of Tai Chi movements are valued for different reasons. For example, Gentle Path Tai Chi movement builds up your energy or qi. Sky Journey Tai Chi motivates you to move gracefully. Infinite Expansion Tai Chi trains you to be naturally in perfect control of your body and physical energy. It is good exercise, but it is a little stronger than Sky Journey and Gentle Path. Harmony Tai Chi balances the energy of all three energy centers.

Tai Chi movement has become more popular than Ba Gua Zhang or Cosmic Tour among the last generation of scholars. The movements are still equally valuable in building health, which is to say, they have a similar healing power as Tai Chi, but the energy flow is different.

Qigong is for health. Dao-In and Eight Treasures are for longevity. Push hands and martial arts are for practical purposes of competition. Sword practice is for spiritual concentration and total integration.

I respect the art that I do. I continue to practice it, because it strengthens my physical being and leads to the attainment of an intangible, immortal life.

Many years ago some students in Taiwan asked why I made the decision to come to the United States. My answer was that only after the ancient arts are accepted by Westerners will the Chinese rediscover what they have devalued and neglected in their own culture. Qi exercise and spiritual learning have both started to generate interest in China now.

15 Harmony Tai Chi: Warm Up

The Eight Treasures Warm Up

This Warm-Up sequence is called "The Eight Treasures Warm-Up" because it is usually done prior to performing the Eight Treasures Qi-Gong - an ancient system of energy enhancement exercises comprising 32-64 movements[1]. Traditionally, in our family tradition, the Eight Treasures were learned prior to studying Tai Chi.

The Warm-Up is very important prior to starting Tai Chi because it activates the flow of qi in all parts of the body, and is also good for relieving stress. The Warm-Up may also be done by itself to promote energy circulation at any time during the day.

The Warm-Up starts in the tan tien. "Tan tien" is the term for the energy centers of the body. The lower tan tien is located in the abdomen, about two inches below the navel. It is very important in Tai Chi. Also of some importance are the middle tan tien, located at the "heart center" or in the center of the chest, and the upper tan tien between the eyebrows.

The Warm-Up also focuses on the kidney area, slightly above the waist on both sides of the spine.

1. Awakening Qi in the Channels

These warm-up movements help to awaken or activate qi in the energy channels of the body.

A. Tapping the trunk

Start with the feet shoulder-width apart. Let your arms hang down at the sides of the body. Relax your body, especially the neck and shoulder muscles. Initiate a turning movement by shifting your weight from side to side, turning at the waist and pelvic area to cause your arms to swing. With loose fists, gently tap the area below your waist (slightly below the level of your navel) in front and back, which is called the lower tan tien. The gentle weight shift or rocking from side to side helps give momentum to your arm swings.

Continue tapping the trunk lightly, gradually moving the fists up the chest in a "V" pattern to your shoulders.

Gradually backtrack down the same path, returning to the lower tan tien. Repeat a few times.

BREATHING: Breathe deeply and naturally.

B. Tapping the trunk and arms

Start with the feet shoulder-width apart. Make a loose fist with the right hand, lift and extend the left arm, and tap from the level of the navel to under the arm, up the shoulder to the neck, down the shoulder, down the inside of the arm to the palm, back up the outside of the arm, and in along the shoulder to the neck.

Repeat on the other side with the left hand and right arm.

BREATHING: Breathe deeply and naturally.

C. Tapping the back and legs

Start with the feet wide apart (the width of the horse stance, but with legs straight). Making loose fists with the hands, bend forward at the waist and tap with the backs of the fists in circles over the kidneys, moving up the spine, out to the sides, down the sides, and back in to the spine, circling a few times.

Continue tapping with the insides of the fists along the sides of the buttocks, down the outside of the legs to the ankles, switch to the inside of the ankles and tap up the inside of the legs to the connection of the legs to the trunk (the ligaments on each side of the crotch).

Bring the feet in to shoulder-width apart, and tap with the inside of loose fists against the connection of the legs to the trunk, alternating with legs straight and legs bent a few times, giving an up and down motion while tapping.

BREATHING: Deep and natural.

D. Swinging the arms back and jumping up

Start with the feet shoulder-width apart. Freely swing the arms from front to back until you find the point of natural resistance in back and then let them swing to the front again.

After several swings, to enhance the movement, bend the knees slightly and lift the heels as the arms swing back and up.

After several more swings, jump up as the arms swing back and up. Feel as though the momentum of your arms swinging back carries you up. Repeat, going progressively higher each time.

Then, gradually jump less and less high, slow down and gradually stop swinging the arms, bending the knees and lifting the heels, and return to a normal standing position.

BREATHING: Inhale when arms swing back and up.

2. <u>Loosening and Opening up the Joints</u>

These warm-up movements loosen and open up the major joints of the body, allowing qi to pass through them more easily. Several optional movements are also included to open up the remaining joints of the body.

A. Turning the neck

Start with heels together and hands together. Men place right hand underneath left hand, women place left hand underneath right hand. Place the thumb of the upper hand inside the thumb of the lower hand, and the first joint of one of the fingers of the upper hand over the side of the big knuckle of the little finger on the lower hand.

Keeping the neck relaxed, slightly bend the upper body and shoulders to allow gravity to roll the head gently and slowly to the left, back to the right, and front in a circle, repeating several times.

Reverse direction when the head is bent forward, and repeat.

BREATHING: Inhale as your head circles to the back, exhale as it circles to the front.

B. (optional) Turning the shoulders

Keeping the arms relaxed, lift the left shoulder and turn the waist to roll the shoulder from front to back, repeating a few times. Reverse, lifting the shoulder back to front, repeating a few more times.

Repeat on the other side.

NOTE: As an alternative, big shoulder rotations can be done. Lift the arm on the left side straight up above the shoulder and rotate it down in front and up in back, circling a few times. Reverse direction, circling a few more times. Repeat on the other side.

BREATHING: Inhale when circling up and exhale when circling down.

C. (optional) Turning the elbows

Place the right hand over the elbow area in front of the left arm hanging down at the side. Keeping the hand loosely over the elbow area, bend the left arm up at the elbow, turning it up toward the body on the inside of the right arm, and then circle the left forearm back down away from the body. Repeat a few times.

Reverse direction, bending the left arm at the elbow and turning it up away from the body and back down towards the body to circle inside the right arm.

Repeat on the other side.

BREATHING: Inhale when circling up and exhale when circling down.

D. (optional) Turning the wrists

Keeping the arms relaxed and hanging down at the sides, turn the hands around the wrist on each side, a few times toward the trunk in front, then reverse for a few more times away from the trunk in front.

Gently shake the hands, then the hands and lower arms, then the hands and lower and upper arms.

NOTE: As an alternative, clasp the hands with fingers interlaced and trace a "figure eight" in front of the body. Try to get a full range of motion when turning and bending the wrists. After repeating a few times, reverse direction for a few more times.

BREATHING: Breathe deeply and naturally.

E. (optional) Turning the waist

Start with feet wide apart (the width of a horse stance, but with legs straight). Place the hands on the waist on each side, and bend forward at the waist. Keeping the hands in place and turning at the waist, circle the upper body around to the left, lean back, to the right, and bend forward again, repeating a few times. When bent forward, reverse direction and repeat a few more times, then straighten up.

BREATHING: Inhale when circling to the back, exhale when circling to the front.

F. Turning the hips

Start with heels together, or farther apart if necessary for balance. Place the palms of the hands over the kidneys and rub them a few times to warm them up.

Keeping the palms over the kidneys, and the head upright and over the feet, push the hips forward, then to the left, back, to the right, and forward to make a complete rotation. Repeat several times.

Reverse direction and repeat several more times in the opposite direction, then straighten up.

BREATHING: Exhale as the hips circle forward, inhale back.

G. Turning the knees

Start with feet together. Bend forward at the waist and rest the hands on the knees. Lightly rub the knees to warm them. Make a circle by bending the knees to the left, then in front and to the right, and then straighten them. Repeat several times. Reverse the direction of the circles and repeat several more times.

Next, make circles by bending the knees forward and separating them, moving them out to each side, and circling back as you straighten them. Repeat several more times.

Reverse the direction of the circles and repeat.

BREATHING: Exhale when knees bend down, inhale when straightening up.

H. Turning the ankles

Lift the left foot. Rotate it at the ankle several times in one direction, then in the other. Alternate pointing and flexing the foot, then shake it to loosen the ankle joint. Repeat for the other foot.

NOTE: An alternative to loosen the ankle joint is to place the left foot at an angle behind you, ball of the foot on the ground and heel in the air. Turn that foot's ankle in big circles, then reverse the direction of the circles. Repeat on the other side.

BREATHING: Deep and natural.

16 Harmony Tai Chi: Basic Stances

Basic Stances

There are several basic stances in Harmony Style Tai Chi that should be learned by the beginner: the horse stance, cat stance, heel stance, bow (or front) stance, twist stance, and half-step stance.

The Horse Stance – The horse stance is done with feet shoulder-width apart, feet pointing straight ahead, knees bent, waist loose, pelvis tucked in, and shoulders relaxed. The body weight is evenly distributed (50/50) across both feet.

The Cat Stance – The cat stance is done with 90% of the weight on the rear foot which is angled at 45 degrees. The front foot is pointed straight ahead with 10% of the weight and touching the ground with the ball of the foot. The knees are bent. The centerline of the body faces the diagonal.

The Heel Stance – The heel stance is done with 90% of the weight on the rear foot which is angled at 45 degrees (as in the Cat Stance). The front foot is pointed straight ahead with 10% of the weight but it touches the ground with the heel of the foot. The knees are bent. The centerline of the body faces the diagonal.

The Bow (or Front) Stance – is done with the front foot pointing straight ahead carrying 70% of the body's weight and the rear foot pointing at a 45° angle and carrying 30% of the weight. There should be some space between the front and rear heel. They should not be on the same line. The front knee is bent. The rear knee is almost straight. The trunk of the body faces the same direction as the front foot.

The Twist Stance – is often a transition step between two other stances. For example, this stance often occurs after a cat stance. In this case, the lead foot of the cat stance would lift off the ground, move forward a little, and then touch the ground with the heel first and then with the rest of the foot twisting outward. As weight is transferred to the front foot, the rear foot would come up on the ball of the foot as it prepares to move into the next stance.

The Half-Step Stance – is often used after the twist stance before going into another stance like the bow stance. In the half-step, one foot is flat on the ground with 80% of the weight. The other foot touches the ground with the ball of the foot next to the heel of the first foot with 20% of the weight.

Tai Chi Stepping – When moving from one stance to another, a step is taken in which the lead foot touches the ground (heel first) initially "empty" or with "no weight." Then the rest of the foot is set down with "no weight." After the whole foot is on the ground, then weight is gradually transferred to the lead foot. In the sequence above, the empty step occurs as a transition between the cat stance and the bow (or front) stance. All stepping in Tai Chi involves the empty step, in which one steps with no weight and then, when the lead foot is planted, weight is transferred (the percentage of weight will vary with the stance).

17 18-Step Harmony Tai Chi-Short Form

The purpose of the 18-Step Harmony Tai Chi Short Form is to provide an opportunity for students to begin their studies of Harmony Tai Chi – a unique style never before taught outside of the Integral Way Tradition. With the 18-Step Harmony Tai Chi Short Form, students are introduced to the spiritual names of each tai chi movement. For example, "Cloud Hands" in the Integral Way Tradition is also known as "Move Without Exhaustion." The movement "Single Whip" is also known as "Exposition of the Heavenly Mystery". These spiritual names embody principles and virtues which are taught in the various chapters of Lao Tzu's *Tao Te Ching*. Thus, students become aware that Harmony Tai Chi is a perfect practice for experiencing the profoundness of the Tao. Harmony Tai Chi is like the rhythmic dance of the four seasons – Sprouting, Expanding, Harvesting and Returning to the Root, and then the seasonal cycle repeats endlessly.

Both the beginner's 18-Step Harmony Tai Chi Short Form and the intermediate 28-Step Harmony Tai Chi Form may be used profitably as a daily practice. For those seeking the most helpful way to cultivate their qi or energy, the complete set of yin/yang movements is found in the advanced 108-Step Harmony Tai Chi Long Form.

18-Step Harmony Tai Chi

(Beginner's Form)

Common Names	Spiritual Names
0. Wu Chi	The Great Void
1. Beginning Tai Chi	Existence Before Heaven and Earth
2. Grasp the Sparrow's Tail	The Gate of Subtle Origin
a. Brush Sleeve – R	Raise the Lower
b. Roll Back	Lower the Elevated
c. Press	Decrease the Overabundant

d. Push

Nourish the Insufficient

3. Double Whip

Exposition of the Heavenly Mystery

(Yang Within Yin)

4. Brush Knee – L

Empty and Yet Productive

5. Playing the Lute – L

The Greatly Skilled Seems Clumsy

6. Brush Knee – R

Empty and Yet Productive

7. Playing the Lute – R

The Greatly Skilled Seems Clumsy

8. Fist Under Elbow

To be Curled is to be Straight

9. Repulse the Monkey (stationary 2x, retreating 3x)

To Progress in Tao Seems Like Regressing

10. Stir the Whirlpool

Draw from the Inexhaustible Source

11. Search for Needle at Bottom of Sea

The Feminine Yin can Overcome the

Masculine Yang

12. Diagonal Flying/Cross Hands in Twist Stance

Straight but not Offensive

13. Twist One Step Fist

To be Brave is to be Kind (One Step)

14. Move Block Fist – R

Within There is Essence

15. Withdraw and Push

Knowing When to Stop is to be Safe

16. Cloud Hands (stationary – 3x)

Move without Exhaustion

17. Cross Hands

Always Embrace the Source

18. Completion of Tai Chi

Return to the Root

0. Wu Chi

The Great Void

18-Step Harmony Tai Chi - Foot Diagram

Legend

This diagram describes the directional terms and angles that are used in the following descriptions for each movement. In the photos that follow, Dr. Mao begins the form by facing the "front." The "right" on the diagram corresponds to his "right" as he faces the "front." This should allow you to use the diagram to understand the directions depicted and described for each movement.

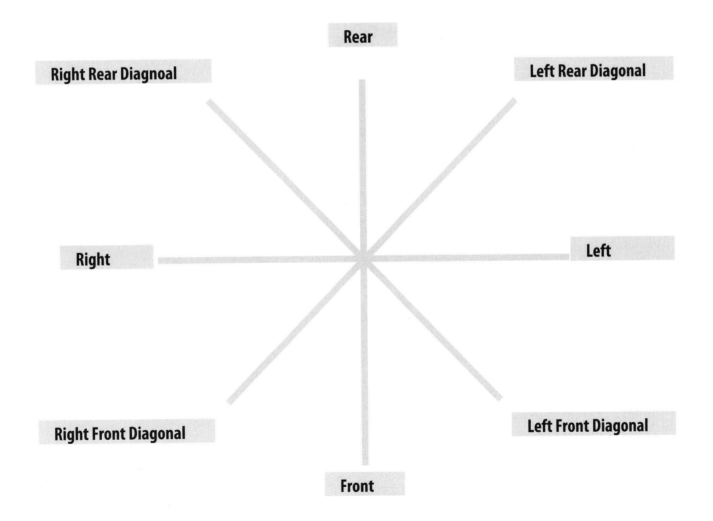

Rear

Right Rear Diagnoal

Left Rear Diagonal

Right

Left

Right Front Diagonal

Left Front Diagonal

Front

Movement 0: Wu Chi

Spiritual Name: The Great Void

0.

The opening stance is called "The Great Void". It symbolizes the unmanifested energy (creative stillness, great void, primal female, or mysterious "mother" aspect) of the Tao. Stand in a horse stance facing the front with knees slightly bent, waist and shoulders relaxed, face forward, chin slightly tucked in, hands down to the sides, pelvis rotated down and forward (as if getting ready to sit down), and mind clear. Curl the tongue so that the bottom of the tip is touching the roof of the mouth.

Movement 1: Beginning Tai Chi

Spiritual Name: Existence Before Heaven and Earth

This is the first movement of the Harmony Style Tai Chi form which has the general function of activating the main energy centers of the body (lower, middle, and upper tan tien) and connecting them to each other and to the environment.

1a	1b	1c	1d	1e	1f
While in the horse stance facing the front, raise both hands slowly with elbows slightly bent to waist level (slightly above lower tan tien).	Return your hands slowly to the sides.	Raise both hands slowly to the eyebrow level (above middle tan tien level).	Bring hands inward toward the heart (middle tan tien) level and push them straight out. Do not lock the elbows when extending the arms straight out.	Return hands toward top of head level (above upper tan tien). Stop when hands are about 6 inches in front of head. Face palms toward front with fingers pointing to sky.	Let your hands descend slowly to the sides.

Movement 2: Grasp the Sparrow's Tail

Spiritual Name: Gate of Subtle Origin

"Mini Cloud Hands Transition"

Brush Sleeve (or Ward Off)

Spiritual Name: Raise the Lower

2a	2b	2c	2d	2e
In the horse stance, turn your body to the right front diagonal. Circle your right hand (palm down) up and outward to the right at shoulder level. At the same time, turn your left hand palm up and bring it to the waist. Both hands should now be positioned as if holding a "ball" of energy. Shift your weight 60% to the right foot.	Turn your body to the left front diagonal. Circle your left hand up and outward at shoulder level to the left with palm down. At the same time, turn your right hand palm up and bring it to the waist. Shift your weight 60% to the left foot.	Rotate the left foot outward (pivot on the heel) to the left front diagonal. Then shift your weight to the left foot and bring your right foot up close to the left heel to form a half-step stance.	Step out with your right foot to form a right bow stance on the right front diagonal.	While forming a right bow stance, rotate your left foot to the front (pivot on the heel). Bring your right arm forward, from under your left arm (as if brushing the left sleeve), to chest level with palm facing the body. At the same time, bring your left hand down towards the left knee with palm parallel to the ground.

Movement 2: Grasp the Sparrow's Tail (continued)

Roll Back

Spiritual Name: Lower the Elevated

2f	2g	2h	2i	2j

2f	**2g**	**2h**	**2i**	**2j**
From the previous position, circle your left hand out and to the front with palm up.	Then turn both hands palms down and swing both arms to the left across thighs and shift your weight to your left foot while rotating your right foot (pivoting on heel) to the left front diagonal.	At the end of the arm swing, your left palm and elbow should be facing the left. Your right palm should be facing up and positioned near the lower tan tien. The weight should be on the left foot and the right foot should be rotated to face the left front diagonal.	Shift your weight to your right foot and bring your left foot up to form a cat stance facing the left. The left palm and elbow should still be facing the left. The body should be facing the left front diagonal.	Now circle your left hand close to the body up to the middle tan tien by bending at the elbow (do not raise the left shoulder). At the same time, turn the body to the left and bring the right hand to the middle tan tien. The right palm should rest on the left wrist.

Movement 2: Grasp the Sparrow's Tail (continued)

Press	Push
Spiritual Name: Decrease the Overabundant	**Spiritual Name: Nourish the Insufficient**

2k	2l	2m	2n	2o
Press your hands forward from the middle of the chest as you step out with your left foot to form a bow stance facing the left. The left arm should be horizontal to the ground. The base of the right palm should contact the left wrist.	Continue to press your hands forward while coming into a bow stance. The hands should not extend beyond the front knee. The left arm should be horizontal.	From the left bow stance, transfer your weight to the rear foot and come back into a left cat stance. At the same time, brush your left arm from the shoulder to the hand with your right hand. The whole hand should extend over the left arm in this brushing motion.	Circle both hands up and back toward the forehead and then to the heart and middle tan tien level.	Step out into a bow stance facing the left and at the same time, push both hands forward from the waist in an upward semi-arc to chest level. Hands should not extend beyond front knee.

Movement 3: Double Whip

Spiritual Name: Exposition of the Heavenly Mystery (Yang Within Yin)

This movement is unique to Harmony Tai Chi. The common name for this movement is "double whip."

3a	3b	3c	3d

From the left bow stance, shift the weight onto the rear leg as you rotate (pivot on heel) the left foot to the front. At the same time, the body and arms also circle toward the front with left palm up and right palm down.

When the arms have reached the front, shift your weight to the left leg and bring the right foot close to the left heel to form a half-step stance facing the front. At the same time, form a crane's beak with the left hand with all five fingers touching and facing downward. Position the right hand with an open palm (fingers facing upward) near the left hand's crane beak.

Scoop the right hand down and in towards the body and bring it palm up close to the left ear.

Circle the right hand horizontally outward and to the right (palm up). At the same time, open the left hand, turn it palm up, and circle it to the right under the right arm towards the right arm pit. While the arms circle, turn the right foot to the right, set it flat on the ground, and transfer your weight to it. Raise up the left heel and rotate on the ball of the foot so that the left foot is now aligned with the right front diagonal.

Movement 3: Double Whip (continued)

Spiritual Name: Exposition of the Heavenly Mystery (Yang Within Yin)

3e	3f	3g	3h

At full extension of this circling motion, the right palm should be up, the left palm should be face up and under the right arm pit. The arms should circle as far as the right rear diagonal.

Now bring the right arm close to the body and pull the left hand through the right armpit. At the same time, shift your weight to the rear leg to form a cat facing the right. The hands should meet at the middle tan tien (in front of the heart) with the left palm edge resting on the right wrist. The right palm should be vertical and facing the right front diagonal.

With the hands in this position, step out with the right leg. Push the connected hands straight out from the body.

Transfer your weight to the right leg and come into a bow stance facing the right. The connected hands should not extend beyond the front knee. The right palm should still be facing the right front diagonal.

Movement 4: Brush Knee - L

Spiritual Name: Empty and Yet Productive

"Transition"   **"Brush Knee"**

4a	4b	4c	4d	4e
From the right bow stance, shift your weight back to the rear leg to form a cat stance facing the right. At the same time, let the arms descend to hip level and then raise them to shoulder level, palms down, so that they are extended. Elbows should be bent when arms are extended.	Step out with the right foot to form a twist stance. Transfer your weight to the right leg. As weight is slowly transferred to the right leg, turn the right palm up and bring it toward the body. At the same time, bring the left palm past the left ear and toward the right retracting palm.	Brush the left palm (palm down) past the right palm (palm up) and extend the left arm forward. At the same time, raise the left heel.	Step up with the left foot to form a half-step stance (weight should be shifted to the right leg). At the same time, circle the left arm in toward the body and circle the right arm up toward the right ear.	Step out with the left leg to form a bow stance facing the right. At the same time, the left hand circles down and brushes to the side of the left knee, while the right hand extends forward opposite the right shoulder. The right hand should not extend beyond the left knee.

Movement 5: Playing the Lute - L

Spiritual Name: The Greatly Skilled Seems Clumsy

5a	5b	5c	5d	5e
Rock your weight onto the left foot and lift the right heel.	Then shift your weight back to the right foot to form a flat-footed cat stance facing the right. At the same time, bring the left arm up to the right so that they overlap horizontally with the right arm over the left. Arms should be at shoulder level.	Separate arms horizontally outward and then circle them downward (as if scooping up energy from the earth). During downward circling, bend the knees while keeping the back straight.	At the bottom of the circle, the hands, with palms up, should cross at the wrists with the right hand over the left.	Raise the arms up and bring them into guard position with the left arm in front (bent at 45° angle) and the right open hand near the left elbow. At the same time, lift up the front foot and then set it down to form a heel stance facing the right.

Movement 6: Brush Knee - R

Spiritual Name: Empty and Yet Productive

"Transition"			"Brush Knee"	

6a	6b	6c	6d	6e
From the left heel stance, let the arms descend to hip level and then raise them to shoulder level, palms down, so that they are extended. Elbows should be bent when arms are extended. At the same time, rise up on the ball of the left foot to form a cat stance.	Step out with the left foot to form a twist stance. Transfer your weight to the left leg. As weight is slowly transferred to the left leg, turn the left palm up and bring it toward the body. At the same time, bring the right palm past the left ear and toward the left retracting palm.	Brush the right palm (palm down) past the left palm (palm up) and extend the right arm forward. At the same time, raise the right heel.	Step up with the right foot to form a half-step stance (weight should be shifted to the left leg). At the same time, circle the right arm in toward the body and circle the left arm up toward the right ear.	Step out with the right leg to form a bow stance facing the right. At the same time, the right hand circles down and brushes to the side of the right knee, while the left hand extends forward opposite the left shoulder. The left hand should not extend beyond the left knee.

Movement 7: Playing the Lute - R

Spiritual Name: The Greatly Skilled Seems Clumsy

7a	7b	7c	7d	7e
Rock your weight onto the right foot and lift the left heel.	Then shift your weight back to the left foot to form a flat-footed cat stance facing the right. At the same time, bring the right arm up to the left so that they overlap horizontally with the left arm over the right. Arms should be at shoulder level.	Separate arms horizontally outward and then circle them downward (as if scooping up energy from the earth). During downward circling, bend the knees while keeping the back straight.	At the bottom of the circle, the hands, with palms up, should cross at the wrists with the left hand over the right.	Raise the arms up and bring them into guard position with the right arm in front (bent at 45° angle) and the left open hand near the right elbow. At the same time, lift up the front foot and then set it down to form a heel stance facing the right.

Movement 8: Fist Under Elbow

Spiritual Name: To Be Curled is to Be Straight

8a

From the heel stance, lift your right hand and elbow slightly. At the same time, form a vertical fist with your left hand and place it under the right elbow and lift the front foot and set it down to form a cat stance facing the right.

8b

Step forward with your right foot and bring your left vertical fist forward from under your right elbow.

Movement 9: Repulse the Monkey - Stationary

Spiritual Name: To Progress in Tao Seems Like Regressing

Stationary – 2 times (counted as palms passing each other twice)

9a	9b	9c	9d
As you complete your left punch, bring your left foot up into a horse stance facing the right. Your right hand should extend toward the rear.	Then turn the palms upward and bring the right hand forward near the right ear while retracting the left hand towards the body. At the same time, turn the body at the waist to face forward.	Continue to draw the left arm toward the rear (at chest level). At the same time, brush the right palm past the left palm.	Extend the right palm forward while moving the left arm down toward the waist (palm up) and then extending it behind the body (palm down).

Movement 9: Repulse the Monkey - Stationary (continued)

9e

At full extension, turn the right and left palms face down and the turn the body at the waist to the right front diagonal.

9f

Then turn the palms upward and bring the left hand forward near the left ear while retracting the right hand towards the body. At the same time, turn the body at the waist to face the right.

9g

Continue to draw the right arm towards the body (at chest level). At the same time, brush the left palm past the right palm.

9h

Extend the left arm forward while moving the right arm down toward the waist (palm up) and then extending it behind the body.

Movement 9: Repulse the Monkey - Retreating

Spiritual Name: To Progress in Tao Seems Like Regressing

Retreating – 3 times

9i	9j	9k	9l
At full extension, turn the left and right palms face down and turn the body at the waist to the right rear diagonal.	From the previous position, shift your weight onto the right foot and bring your left foot close to the right heel to form a half-step stance.	Step back with your left leg (touching the ground toe first), turn the left palm up, and bring your right palm close to the right ear.	Transfer your weight to the left foot to form a cat stance facing the right. At the same time, turn the body to the left and brush your right hand past the right ear and then left palm.

Movement 9: Repulse the Monkey - Retreating (continued)

9m	9n	9o	9p

Extend your right hand past the left palm. The right palm should face forward. The left palm should be up.

Withdraw your left arm behind the body. Extend both arms with palms down. Elbows should not be locked. The body's centerline should face the right front diagonal.

Step back with your right leg (touching the ground toe first), turn the right palm up, and bring your left palm close to the left ear.

Transfer your weight to the right foot to form a cat stance facing the right. At the same time, turn the body to the right rear diagonal and brush your left hand past the left ear and then right palm.

Movement 9: Repulse the Monkey - Retreating (continued)

9q	9r	9s	9t	9u
Extend your left hand past the right palm. The left palm should face forward. The right palm should be up.	Withdraw your right arm behind the body. Extend both arms with palms down. Elbows should not be locked. The body's centerline should face the right rear diagonal.	Step back with your left leg (touching the ground toe first), turn the left palm up, and bring your right palm close to the right ear.	Transfer your weight to the left foot to form a cat stance facing the right. At the same time, turn the body to the right and brush your right hand past the right ear and then left palm.	Extend your right hand past the left palm. The right palm should face forward. The left palm should be up.

Movement 10: Stir the Whirlpool

Spiritual Name: Draw from the Inexhaustible Source

10a

Withdraw your left arm to the rear. Extend both arms with palms down. Elbows should not be locked. You should be in a right cat stance. The body's centerline should face the right front diagonal.

10b

While remaining in a cat stance, let the hands descend, palms up, to the left hip.

10c

Now step out with the right foot to form a bow stance facing the right and circle both hands out and to the right, turning palms down. Hands should circle up to the upper tan tien level.

10d

Turn the palms up and bring them toward the lower tan tien. At the same time, shift your weight to the left foot.

10e

Bring the right foot close to the left heel to form a half-step stance. The hands should be palms up at the left hip (right palm over left palm).

Movement 11: Search for the Needle at the Bottom of the Sea

Spiritual Name: The Feminine Yin Can Overcome the Masculine Yang

11a

Step back with the right foot along the right rear diagonal and bring the left foot close to the right foot to form a half-step stance with toes pointed toward the right front diagonal. Your weight should now be on the right foot. At the same time, turn the left palm down and circle the hands out to the right at middle tan tien level.

11b

As the hands circle around to the right, bring the left arm under the right arm. The right palm faces upward and is positioned near the left shoulder. The left palm faces down and reaches toward the outside of the right knee.

Movement 12: Diagonal Flying/Cross Hands in Twist Stance

Spiritual Name: Straight But Not Offensive

REAR VIEW   FRONT VIEW

12a	12b	12c	12d

12a

Step out with the left foot to the front to form a left bow stance. As you transfer your weight to the left foot, rotate the right foot (pivot on the heel) to the front. At the same time, the left palm turns up and brushes past the right palm. The left arm extends upward and outward to about face level, while the right arm extends backward to the rear to about hip level.

12b

Then, step up with the right foot (as if forming a horse stance) and then transfer your weight to it. Rotate the body to the left while rotating the left foot outward (pivoting on the heel).

12c

When the left foot reaches the left rear diagonal, then set it flat on the ground and transfer your weight to it while lifting up your right heel. At the same time, continue to rotate your body so that it faces the rear.

12d

As the body comes to face the rear, cross the right arm in front of the left arm and bring them together at the wrists. The palms should be facing outward to the sides and the crossed arms should be in front of the middle tan tien. Bend the knees to the degree that is comfortable.

Movement 13: Twist One Step Fist

Spiritual Name: To Be Brave is to Be Kind

13a	13b	13c	13d
From the previous position, straighten the knees (but do not fully extend), and let the hands descend.	Then step out with the right leg into a twist stance while the body and arms begin to swing out to the front.	Transfer the weight to the right foot and step up with the left foot into a half-step stance. As the arms swing to the front, the left palm should be up and the right arm should move behind the body with palm facing downward.	Close the right hand into a horizontal fist. Turn the left palm to face the body.

Movement 14: Move Block Fist

Spiritual Name: Within There is Essence

14a

Step out with left foot. Turn the right fist from a horizontal to a vertical fist. Bring it forward past the right hip as you punch forward. Turn the left palm downward and begin moving it toward the right fist.

14b

Transfer your weight to your left leg to form a bow stance. Bring your right fist forward to knee level. Bring your left palm and rest it, palm down, on the right wrist.

Movement 15: Withdraw and Push

Spiritual Name: Knowing When to Stop is to be Safe

15a	15b	15c	15d	15e
From the bow stance, rock your weight to the front foot and lift the heel of the rear foot.	Shift your weight to the rear leg as the left front leg withdraws back to form a left cat stance. At the same time, tuck your left hand (palm down) under the right arm pit and sweep it forward under the right arm. When the left arm reaches the right elbow it turns palm up.	When the left hand reaches the right hand, the hands will be crossed at the wrist (left hand over right) with palms facing the body at chest level. Separate the hands to the sides forming a horizontal circling motion.	Circle the hands in toward the middle tan tien. As the hands come in toward the chest, the palms turn to face outward.	Step out with the left foot to form a bow stance and push the hands forward. The hands should not extend beyond the front knee.

Movement 16: Cloud Hands - Stationary

Spiritual Name: Move Without Exhaustion

16a	**16b**	**16c**
From the left bow stance, rotate the rear foot to the front and then transfer your weight to it. Then bring the left foot up into a horse stance facing the front.	While in the horse stance, turn your body to the right front diagonal as you circle the right hand up and outward at shoulder level to the right with palm down. The elbow should be lower than the wrist. At the same time, turn your left hand palm up and bring it to the lower tan tien. Both hands should now be positioned as if holding a "ball" of energy. Shift your weight 60% to the right foot.	Turn your body to the left front diagonal as you circle the left hand up and outward at shoulder level to the left with palm down. The elbow should be lower than the wrist. At the same time, turn your right hand palm up and bring it to the lower tan tien level. Shift your weight 60% to the left foot. Repeat b & c two more times.

Movement 17: Cross Hands

Spiritual Name: Always Embrace the Source

| 17a | 17b | 17c |

From the last cloud hands position, while the left hand is still up, bring the right arm up to the left and then separate them as you circle them outward to the sides and then downward.

As you circle the arms downward, bend the knees. The motion of the hands are as if one is scooping energy from the earth. Keep the back straight. At the bottom of the circle, cross the hands (left over right) at the wrists.

Bring the crossed hands up in front of the middle tan tien (heart level). Palms should face the sides.

Movement 18: Completion of Tai Chi

Spiritual Name: Return to the Root

18a

18b

18c

18d

From the cross hands position, uncross the hands and let them descend in front of the body toward the thighs.

Turn the hands palms up and circle them out and toward the front, with elbows bent, to the level of the shoulders.

Let the hands descend slowly in front of the body toward the thighs.

Once the hands are at the thighs, the knees are still bent.

Movement 0: Wu Chi

Spiritual Name: The Great Void

0

Now let the hands move to the sides and straighten the knees. The ending stance is the same as the beginning stance. The form ends where it begins. This embodies the principle that the manifested energy (yin and yang) of the Tao ultimately returns to the creative stillness of Wu Chi – the unmanifested subtle essence of the Tao.

Closing Movement

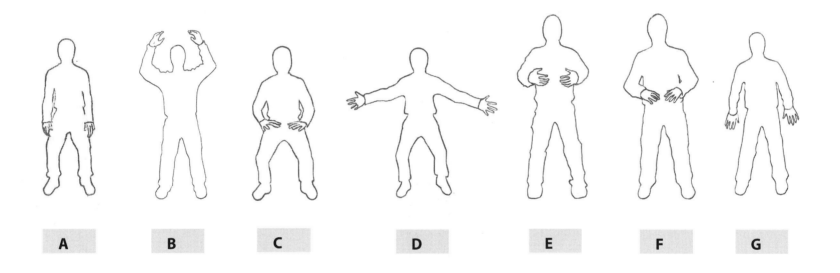

| A | B | C | D | E | F | G |

When Tai Chi practice is finished, it is important to perform a closing movement in order to draw the expanded energy (generated during Tai Chi practice) back down into the lower tan tien for storage. This can be done in a horse stance with knees slightly bent and arms down at the sides (Fig. A). Slowly circle the arms outward and upward. When they reach the overhead position, palms should be facing downward (Fig. B). Slowly let the arms descend (palms down) in front of the body toward the lower tan tien (Fig. C). When they reach the sides, circle the arms horizontally outward and toward the front at the level of the lower tan tien (Fig. D). When the arms reach the front, palms should be facing toward the body. Then slowly bring the hands toward the lower tan tien. Stop when the palms are about 12 inches from the lower tan tien. Remain in this position for a few minutes (Fig. E). This is the Tai Chi standing meditation position. Then turn the palms downward (Fig F) and let the arms descend to the sides as the knees straighten and the feet come together (Fig. G).

BREATHING: As the arms circle outward and upward, inhale. As they descend, exhale. As the arms circle horizontally outward and toward the front, inhale. As they are drawn toward the lower tan tien, exhale. All other times, breathe deeply and naturally.

18 28-Step Harmony Tai Chi-Intermediate Form

The purpose of the 28-Step Harmony Tai Chi Intermediate Form is to provide an opportunity for students who have mastered the beginner's form (18-Step Harmony Tai Chi) to further their studies of Harmony Tai Chi. The 28-Step Harmony Tai Chi Form adds ten additional movements to the 18-Step form. So, once a person knows the beginner's short form, then they already know about two-thirds of intermediate, 28-Step form. The ten new movements include some of the basic kicks of the Yin Section (Part 1) of the advanced 108-Step Harmony Tai Chi Long Form.

Both the beginner's 18-Step Harmony Tai Chi Form and the intermediate 28-Step Harmony Tai Chi Form may be used profitably as a daily practice. For those seeking the most helpful way to cultivate their qi or energy, the complete set of yin/yang movements is found in the advanced 108-Step Harmony Tai Chi Long Form.

28-Step Harmony Tai Chi

(Intermediate Form)

Common Names	Spiritual Names
0. Wu Chi	The Great Void
1. Beginning Tai Chi	Existence Before Heaven and Earth
2. Grasp the Sparrow's Tail	The Gate of Subtle Origin
a. Brush Sleeve – R	Raise the Lower
b. Roll Back	Lower the Elevated
c. Press	Decrease the Overabundant
d. Push	Nourish the Insufficient
3. Double Whip	Exposition of the Heavenly Mystery
	(Yang Within Yin)

4. Brush Knee – L	Empty and Yet Productive
5. Playing the Lute – L	The Greatly Skilled Seems Clumsy
6. Brush Knee – R	Empty and Yet Productive
7. Playing the Lute – R	The Greatly Skilled Seems Clumsy
8. Fist Under Elbow	To be Curled is to be Straight
9. Repulse the Monkey (stationary 2x, retreating 3x)	To Progress in Tao Seems Like Regressing
10. Stir the Whirlpool	Draw from the Inexhaustible Source
11. Search for Needle at Bottom of Sea	The Feminine Yin can Overcome the Masculine Yang
12. Diagonal Flying/Cross Hands in Twist Stance	Straight but not Offensive
13. Twist One Step Fist	To be Brave is to be Kind
14. Move Block Fist	Within There is Essence
15. Withdraw and Push	Knowing When to Stop is to be Safe
16. Cloud Hands (stationary – 3x, to the right 3x)	Move without Exhaustion
17. Double Whip	Exposition of the Heavenly Mystery (Yang Within Yin)
18. Brush Right Palm	Discreet Like a Humble Guest
19. Left and Right Foot Snap Kick	Fording the Stream at Early Spring
20. Left Heel Kick	One Good at Walking Leaves No Traces
21. Twist One Step	To be Brave is to be Kind
22. Left Hand on Wrist	The Great Dwells in a Lowly Position
23. Move Block Fist	Within There is Essence
24. Withdraw and Push	Knowing When to Stop is to be Safe
25. Single Whip	Exposition of the Heavenly Mystery (Yin Within Yang)
26. Cloud Hands (stationary – 3x)	Move without Exhaustion

27. Cross Hands   Always Embrace the Source
28. Completion of Tai Chi   Return to the Root
0. Wu Chi   The Great Void

28-Step Harmony Tai Chi - Foot Diagram

Legend

This diagram describes the directional terms and angles that are used in the following descriptions for each movement. In the photos that follow, Dr. Mao begins the form by facing the "front." The "right" on the diagram corresponds to his "right" as he faces the "front." This should allow you to use the diagram to understand the directions depicted and described for each movement.

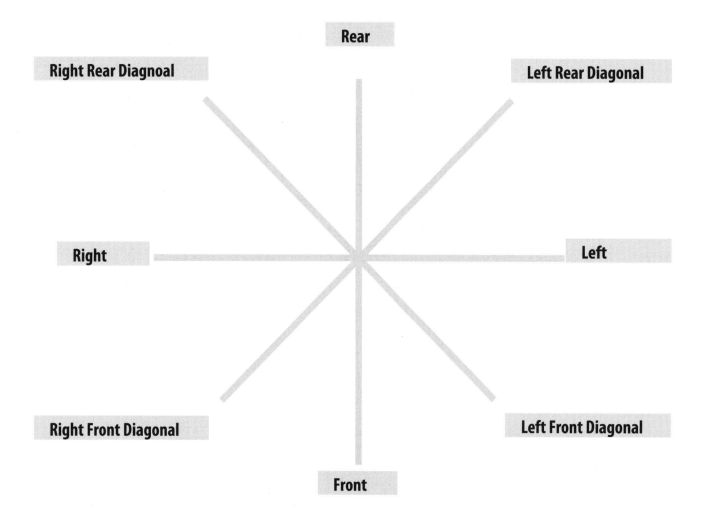

Movement 0: Wu Chi

Spiritual Name: The Great Void

0.

The opening stance is called "The Great Void". It symbolizes the unmanifested energy (creative stillness, great void, primal female, or mysterious "mother" aspect) of the Tao. Stand in a horse stance facing the front with knees slightly bent, waist and shoulders relaxed, face forward, chin slightly tucked in, hands down to the sides, pelvis rotated down and forward (as if getting ready to sit down), and mind clear. Curl the tongue so that the bottom of the tip is touching the roof of the mouth.

Movement 1: Beginning Tai Chi

Spiritual Name: Existence Before Heaven and Earth

This is the first movement of the Harmony Style Tai Chi form which has the general function of activating the main energy centers of the body (lower, middle, and upper tan tien) and connecting them to each other and to the environment.

1a	1b	1c	1d	1e	1f
While in the horse stance facing the front, raise both hands slowly with elbows slightly bent to waist level (slightly above lower tan tien).	Return your hands slowly to the sides.	Raise both hands slowly to the eyebrow level (above middle tan tien level).	Bring hands inward toward the heart (middle tan tien) level and push them straight out. Do not lock the elbows when extending the arms straight out.	Return hands toward top of head level (above upper tan tien). Stop when hands are about 6 inches in front of head. Face palms toward front with fingers pointing to sky.	Let your hands descend slowly to the sides.

Movement 2: Grasp the Sparrow's Tail

Spiritual Name: Gate of Subtle Origin

"Mini Cloud Hands Transition"	Brush Sleeve (or Ward Off)
	Spiritual Name: Raise the Lower

2a	2b	2c	2d	2e
In the horse stance, turn your body to the right front diagonal. Circle your right hand (palm down) up and outward to the right at shoulder level. At the same time, turn your left hand palm up and bring it to the waist. Both hands should now be positioned as if holding a "ball" of energy. Shift your weight 60% to the right foot.	Turn your body to the left front diagonal. Circle your left hand up and outward at shoulder level to the left with palm down. At the same time, turn your right hand palm up and bring it to the waist. Shift your weight 60% to the left foot.	Rotate the left foot outward (pivot on the heel) to the left front diagonal. Then shift your weight to the left foot and bring your right foot up close to the left heel to form a half-step stance.	Step out with your right foot to form a right bow stance on the right front diagonal.	While forming a right bow stance, rotate your left foot to the front (pivot on the heel). Bring your right arm forward, from under your left arm (as if brushing the left sleeve), to chest level with palm facing the body. At the same time, bring your left hand down towards the left knee with palm parallel to the ground.

Movement 2: Grasp the Sparrow's Tail (continued)

Roll Back

Spiritual Name: Lower the Elevated

2f	2g	2h	2i	2j
From the previous position, circle your left hand out and to the front with palm up.	Then turn both hands palms down and swing both arms to the left across thighs and shift your weight to your left foot while rotating your right foot (pivoting on heel) to the left front diagonal.	At the end of the arm swing, your left palm and elbow should be facing the left. Your right palm should be facing up and positioned near the lower tan tien. The weight should be on the left foot and the right foot should be rotated to face the left front diagonal.	Shift your weight to your right foot and bring your left foot up to form a cat stance facing the left. The left palm and elbow should still be facing the left. The body should be facing the left front diagonal.	Now circle your left hand close to the body up to the middle tan tien by bending at the elbow (do not raise the left shoulder). At the same time, turn the body to the left and bring the right hand to the middle tan tien. The right palm should rest on the left wrist.

Movement 2: Grasp the Sparrow's Tail (continued)

Press	Push
Spiritual Name: Decrease the Overabundant	**Spiritual Name: Nourish the Insufficient**

2k	2l	2m	2n	2o
Press your hands forward from the middle of the chest as you step out with your left foot to form a bow stance facing the left. The left arm should be horizontal to the ground. The base of the right palm should contact the left wrist.	Continue to press your hands forward while coming into a bow stance. The hands should not extend beyond the front knee. The left arm should be horizontal.	From the left bow stance, transfer your weight to the rear foot and come back into a left cat stance. At the same time, brush your left arm from the shoulder to the hand with your right hand. The whole hand should extend over the left arm in this brushing motion.	Circle both hands up and back toward the forehead and then to the heart and and middle tan tien level.	Step out into a bow stance facing the left and at the same time, push both hands forward from the waist in an upward semi-arc to chest level. Hands should not extend beyond front knee.

Movement 3: Double Whip

Spiritual Name: Exposition of the Heavenly Mystery (Yang Within Yin)

This movement is unique to Harmony Tai Chi.   The common name for this movement is "double whip."

3a	3b	3c	3d
From the left bow stance, shift the weight onto the rear leg as you rotate (pivot on heel) the left foot to the front. At the same time, the body and arms also circle toward the front with left palm up and right palm down.	When the arms have reached the front, shift your weight to the left leg and bring the right foot close to the left heel to form a half-step stance facing the front. At the same time, form a crane's beak with the left hand with all five fingers touching and facing downward. Position the right hand with an open palm (fingers facing upward) near the left hand's crane beak.	Scoop the right hand down and in towards the body and bring it palm up close to the left ear.	Circle the right hand horizontally outward and to the right (palm up). At the same time, open the left hand, turn it palm up, and circle it to the right under the right arm towards the right arm pit. While the arms circle, turn the right foot to the right, set it flat on the ground, and transfer your weight to it. Raise up the left heel and rotate on the ball of the foot so that the left foot is now aligned with the right front diagonal.

Movement 3: Double Whip (continued)

| 3e | 3f | 3g | 3h |

At full extension of this circling motion, the right palm should be up, the left palm should be face up and under the right arm pit. The arms should circle as far as the right rear diagonal.

Now bring the right arm close to the body and pull the left hand through the right armpit. At the same time, shift your weight to the rear leg to form a cat facing the right. The hands should meet at the middle tan tien (in front of the heart) with the left palm edge resting on the right wrist. The right palm should be vertical and facing the right front diagonal.

With the hands in this position, step out with the right leg. Push the connected hands straight out from the body.

Transfer your weight to the right leg and come into a bow stance facing the right. The connected hands should not extend beyond the front knee. The right palm should still be facing the right front diagonal.

Movement 4: Brush Knee - L

Spiritual Name: Empty and Yet Productive

"Transition"	"Brush Knee"

4a	4b	4c	4d	4e
From the right bow stance, shift your weight back to the rear leg to form a cat stance facing the right. At the same time, let the arms descend to hip level and then raise them to shoulder level, palms down, so that they are extended. Elbows should be bent when arms are extended.	Step out with the right foot to form a twist stance. Transfer your weight to the right leg. As weight is slowly transferred to the right leg, turn the right palm up and bring it toward the body. At the same time, bring the left palm past the left ear and toward the right retracting palm.	Brush the left palm (palm down) past the right palm (palm up) and extend the left arm forward. At the same time, raise the left heel.	Step up with the left foot to form a half-step stance (weight should be shifted to the right leg). At the same time, circle the left arm in toward the body and circle the right arm up toward the right ear.	Step out with the left leg to form a bow stance facing the right. At the same time, the left hand circles down and brushes to the side of the left knee, while the right hand extends forward opposite the right shoulder. The right hand should not extend beyond the left knee.

Movement 5: Playing the Lute - L

Spiritual Name: The Greatly Skilled Seems Clumsy

5a	**5b**	**5c**	**5d**	**5e**
Rock your weight onto the left foot and lift the right heel.	Then shift your weight back to the right foot to form a flat-footed cat stance facing the right. At the same time, bring the left arm up to the right so that they overlap horizontally with the right arm over the left. Arms should be at shoulder level.	Separate arms horizontally outward and then circle them downward (as if scooping up energy from the earth). During downward circling, bend the knees while keeping the back straight.	At the bottom of the circle, the hands, with palms up, should cross at the wrists with the right hand over the left.	Raise the arms up and bring them into guard position with the left arm in front (bent at 45° angle) and the right open hand near the left elbow. At the same time, lift up the front foot and then set it down to form a heel stance facing the right.

Movement 6: Brush Knee - R

Spiritual Name: Empty and Yet Productive

"Transition"	"Brush Knee"

6a	6b	6c	6d	6e
From the left heel stance, let the arms descend to hip level and then raise them to shoulder level, palms down, so that they are extended. Elbows should be bent when arms are extended. At the same time, rise up on the ball of the left foot to form a cat stance.	Step out with the left foot to form a twist stance. Transfer your weight to the left leg. As weight is slowly transferred to the left leg, turn the left palm up and bring it toward the body. At the same time, bring the right palm past the left ear and toward the left retracting palm.	Brush the right palm (palm down) past the left palm (palm up) and extend the right arm forward. At the same time, raise the right heel.	Step up with the right foot to form a half-step stance (weight should be shifted to the left leg). At the same time, circle the right arm in toward the body and circle the left arm up toward the right ear.	Step out with the right leg to form a bow stance facing the right. At the same time, the right hand circles down and brushes to the side of the right knee, while the left hand extends forward opposite the left shoulder. The left hand should not extend beyond the left knee.

Movement 7: Playing the Lute - R

Spiritual Name: The Greatly Skilled Seems Clumsy

7a	7b	7c	7d	7e
Rock your weight onto the right foot and lift the left heel.	Then shift your weight back to the left foot to form a flat-footed cat stance facing the right. At the same time, bring the right arm up to the left so that they overlap horizontally with the left arm over the right. Arms should be at shoulder level.	Separate arms horizontally outward and then circle them downward (as if scooping up energy from the earth). During downward circling, bend the knees while keeping the back straight.	At the bottom of the circle, the hands, with palms up, should cross at the wrists with the left hand over the right.	Raise the arms up and bring them into guard position with the right arm in front (bent at 45° angle) and the left open hand near the right elbow. At the same time, lift up the front foot and then set it down to form a heel stance facing the right.

Movement 8: Fist Under Elbow

Spiritual Name: To Be Curled is to Be Straight

8a

From the heel stance, lift your right hand and elbow slightly. At the same time, form a vertical fist with your left hand and place it under the right elbow and lift the front foot and set it down to form a cat stance facing the right.

8b

Step forward with your right foot and bring your left vertical fist forward from under your right elbow.

Movement 9: Repulse the Monkey - Stationary

Spiritual Name: To Progress in Tao Seems Like Regressing

Stationary – 2 times (counted as palms passing each other twice)

9a	**9b**	**9c**	**9d**
As you complete your left punch, bring your left foot up into a horse stance facing the right. Your right hand should extend toward the rear.	Then turn the palms upward and bring the right hand forward near the right ear while retracting the left hand towards the body. At the same time, turn the body at the waist to face forward.	Continue to draw the left arm toward the rear (at chest level). At the same time, brush the right palm past the left palm.	Extend the right palm forward while moving the left arm down toward the waist (palm up) and then extending it behind the body (palm down).

Movement 9: Repulse the Monkey - Stationary (continued)

| 9e | 9f | 9g | 9h |

At full extension, turn the right and left palms face down and the turn the body at the waist to the right front diagonal.

Then turn the palms upward and bring the left hand forward near the left ear while retracting the right hand towards the body. At the same time, turn the body at the waist to face the right.

Continue to draw the right arm towards the body (at chest level). At the same time, brush the left palm past the right palm.

Extend the left arm forward while moving the right arm down toward the waist (palm up) and then extending it behind the body.

Movement 9: Repulse the Monkey - Retreating

Spiritual Name: To Progress in Tao Seems Like Regressing

Retreating – 3 times

| **9i** | **9j** | **9k** | **9l** |

At full extension, turn the left and right palms face down and turn the body at the waist to the right rear diagonal.

From the previous position, shift your weight onto the right foot and bring your left foot close to the right heel to form a half-step stance.

Step back with your left leg (touching the ground toe first), turn the left palm up, and bring your right palm close to the right ear.

Transfer your weight to the left foot to form a cat stance facing the right. At the same time, turn the body to the left and brush your right hand past the right ear and then left palm.

Movement 9: Repulse the Monkey - Retreating (continued)

9m	**9n**	**9o**	**9p**
Extend your right hand past the left palm. The right palm should face forward. The left palm should be up.	Withdraw your left arm behind the body. Extend both arms with palms down. Elbows should not be locked. The body's centerline should face the right front diagonal.	Step back with your right leg (touching the ground toe first), turn the right palm up, and bring your left palm close to the left ear.	Transfer your weight to the right foot to form a cat stance facing the right. At the same time, turn the body to the right rear diagonal and brush your left hand past the left ear and then right palm.

Movement 9: Repulse the Monkey - Retreating (continued)

9q	9r	9s	9t	9u
Extend your left hand past the right palm. The left palm should face forward. The right palm should be up.	Withdraw your right arm behind the body. Extend both arms with palms down. Elbows should not be locked. The body's centerline should face the right rear diagonal.	Step back with your left leg (touching the ground toe first), turn the left palm up, and bring your right palm close to the right ear.	Transfer your weight to the left foot to form a cat stance facing the right. At the same time, turn the body to the right and brush your right hand past the right ear and then left palm.	Extend your right hand past the left palm. The right palm should face forward. The left palm should be up.

Movement 10: Stir the Whirlpool

Spiritual Name: Draw from the Inexhaustible Source

10a	10b	10c	10d	10e
Withdraw your left arm to the rear. Extend both arms with palms down. Elbows should not be locked. You should be in a right cat stance. The body's centerline should face the right front diagonal.	While remaining in a cat stance, let the hands descend, palms up, to the left hip.	Now step out with the right foot to form a bow stance facing the right and circle both hands out and to the right, turning , palms down. Hands should circle up to the upper tan tien level.	Turn the palms up and bring them toward the lower tan tien. At the same time, shift your weight to the left foot.	Bring the right foot close to the left heel to form a half-step stance. The hands should be palms up at the left hip (right palm over left palm).

Movement 11: Search for the Needle at the Bottom of the Sea

Spiritual Name: The Feminine Yin Can Overcome the Masculine Yang

11a

Step back with the right foot along the right rear diagonal and bring the left foot close to the right foot to form a half-step stance with toes pointed toward the right front diagonal. Your weight should now be on the right foot. At the same time, turn the left palm down and circle the hands out to the right at middle tan tien level.

11b

As the hands circle around to the right, bring the left arm under the right arm. The right palm faces upward and is positioned near the left shoulder. The left palm faces down and reaches toward the outside of the right knee.

Movement 12: Diagonal Flying/Cross Hands in Twist Stance

Spiritual Name: Straight But Not Offensive

REAR VIEW   FRONT VIEW

12a

12b

12c

12d

Step out with the left foot to the front to form a left bow stance. As you transfer your weight to the left foot, rotate the right foot (pivot on the heel) to the front. At the same time, the left palm turns up and brushes past the right palm. The left arm extends upward and outward to about face level, while the right arm extends backward to the rear to about hip level.

Then, step up with the right foot (as if forming a horse stance) and then transfer your weight to it. Rotate the body to the left while rotating the left foot outward (pivoting on the heel).

When the left foot reaches the left rear diagonal, then set it flat on the ground and transfer your weight to it while lifting up your right heel. At the same time, continue to rotate your body so that it faces the rear.

As the body comes to face the rear, cross the right arm in front of the left arm and bring them together at the wrists. The palms should be facing outward to the sides and the crossed arms should be in front of the middle tan tien. Bend the knees to the degree that is comfortable.

Movement 13: Twist One Step Fist

Spiritual Name: To Be Brave is to Be Kind

13a	**13b**	**13c**	**13d**
From the previous position, straighten the knees (but do not fully extend), and let the hands descend.	Then step out with the right leg into a twist stance while the body and arms begin to swing out to the front.	Transfer the weight to the right foot and step up with the left foot into a half-step stance. As the arms swing to the front, the left palm should be up and the right arm should move behind the body with palm facing downward.	Close the right hand into a horizontal fist. Turn the left palm to face the body.

Movement 14: Move Block Fist

Spiritual Name: Within There is Essence

14a

Step out with left foot. Turn the right fist from a horizontal to a vertical fist. Bring it forward past the right hip as you punch forward. Turn the left palm downward and begin moving it toward the right fist.

14b

Transfer your weight to your left leg to form a bow stance. Bring your right fist forward to knee level. Bring your left palm and rest it, palm down, on the right wrist.

Movement 15: Withdraw and Push

Spiritual Name: Knowing When to Stop is to be Safe

15a	15b	15c	15d	15e

From the bow stance, rock your weight to the front foot and lift the heel of the rear foot.

Shift your weight to the rear leg as the left front leg withdraws back to form a left cat stance. At the same time, tuck your left hand (palm down) under the right arm pit and sweep it forward under the right arm. When the left arm reaches the right elbow it turns palm up.

When the left hand reaches the right hand, the hands will be crossed at the wrist (left hand over right) with palms facing the body at chest level. Separate the hands to the sides forming a horizontal circling motion.

Circle the hands in toward the middle tan tien. As the hands come in toward the chest, the palms turn to face outward.

Step out with the left foot to form a bow stance and push the hands forward. The hands should not extend beyond the front knee.

Movement 16: Cloud Hands - Stationary

Spiritual Name: Move Without Exhaustion

16a

From the left bow stance, rotate the rear foot to the front and then transfer your weight to it. Then bring the left foot up into a horse stance facing the front.

16b

While in the horse stance, turn your body to the right front diagonal as you circle the right hand up and outward at shoulder level to the right with palm down. The elbow should be lower than the wrist. At the same time, turn your left hand palm up and bring it to the lower tan tien. Both hands should now be positioned as if holding a "ball" of energy. Shift your weight 60% to the right foot.

16c

Turn your body to the left front diagonal as you circle the left hand up and outward at shoulder level to the left with palm down. The elbow should be lower than the wrist. At the same time, turn your right hand palm up and bring it to the lower tan tien level. Shift your weight 60% to the left foot. Repeat b & c two more times.

Movement 16: Cloud Hands - Moving to the Right 3x

Spiritual Name: Move Without Exhaustion

16d	16e	16f	16g	16h
Circle the left arm down and inward (palm up) and the right arm up and outward (palm down). At the same time, shift the weight to the left foot. Lift the right foot up and step toward the right.	Turn the body at the waist toward the right front diagonal as both hands extend toward the right. At the same time, shift your weight to the right foot.	Circle the right arm down and inward (palm up). Circle the left arm up and outward (palm down). At the same time, turn the body toward the left and step to the right with the left foot to maintain the horse stance. Continue to turn the body toward the left front diagonal as both hands extend toward the left.	Circle the left arm down and inward (palm up) and the right arm up and outward (palm down). At the same time, shift your weight to the left foot. Turn your waist to the right and step toward the right.	Continue to turn the body toward the right front diagonal as both hands extend toward the right. At the same time, shift your weight to the right foot.

Movement 16: Cloud Hands - Moving to the Right 3x (continued)

16i	**16j**	**16k**	**16l**

Circle the right arm down and inward (palm up) and the left arm up and outward (palm down). At the same time, turn the body toward the left and step to the right with the left foot to maintain the horse stance. Continue to turn the body toward the left front diagonal as both hands extend toward the left.

Circle the left arm down and inward (palm up) and the right arm up and outward (palm down). At the same time, shift your weight to the left foot. Turn your body to the right and step to the right with the right foot.

Continue to turn the body toward the right front diagonal as both hands extend toward the right. At the same time, shift your weight to the right foot.

Circle the right arm down and inward (palm up) and the left arm up and outward (palm down). At the same time, turn the body toward the left and step to the right with the left foot to maintain the horse stance. Continue to turn the body toward the left front diagonal as both hands extend toward the left.

Movement 17: Double Whip

Spiritual Name: Exposition of the Heavenly Mystery (Yang Within Yin)

17a	**17b**	**17c**	**17d**
From cloud hands, shift the weight to the right leg as you step out with your left leg. Bring the right hand closer to the left as you begin to form a crane's beak with the left hand.	When the arms have reached the front, shift your weight to the left leg and bring the right foot close to the left heel to form a half-step stance facing the front. At the same time, form a crane's beak with the left hand with all five fingers touching and facing downward. Position the right hand with an open palm (fingers facing upward) near or touching the left hand's crane beak.	Scoop the right hand down and in towards the body and bring it palm up close to the left ear.	Circle the right hand horizontally outward and to the right (palm up). At the same time, open the left hand, turn it palm up, and circle it to the right under the right arm towards the right arm pit. While the arms circle, turn the right foot to the right, set it flat on the ground, and transfer your weight to it. Raise up the left heel and rotate on the ball of the foot so that the left foot is now aligned with the right front diagonal.

Movement 17: Double Whip (continued)

17e	17f	17g	17h

At full extension of this circling motion, the right palm should be up, the left palm should be face up and under the right arm pit. The arms should circle as far as the right rear diagonal.

Now bring the right arm close to the body and pull the left hand through the right arm pit. At the same time, shift your weight to the rear leg to form a cat facing the right. The hands should meet at the middle tan tien (in front of the heart) with the left palm edge resting on the right wrist. The right palm should be vertical and facing the right front diagonal.

With the hands in this position, step out with the right leg. Push the connected hands straight out from the body.

Transfer your weight to the right leg and come into a bow stance facing the right. The connected hands should not extend beyond the front knee. The right palm should still be facing the right front diagonal.

Movement 18: Brush Right Palm

Spiritual Name: Discreet Like a Humble Guest

18a	18b	18c
From the right bow stance of the previous movement, shift your weight back to the rear leg to form a right cat stance. At the same time, extend the hands (palms down).	Turn the right hand palm up and bring the left hand forward past the left ear.	As the left hand passes the left ear, step with the right foot into a twist stance. At the same time, brush the left palm past the right palm.

Movement 19: Left and Right Foot Snap Kick

Spiritual Name: Fording the Stream at Early Spring

19a	19b	19c	19d
From the previous position, step forward with the left leg to form a horse stance facing the right rear diagonal. At the same time, circle both arms out and down.	Continue to circle the arms downward (as if scooping energy from the earth). Bend the knees. At the bottom of the arc, cross the arms at the wrists.	Bring the crossed arms up toward the head. At the head, turn the palms outward and circle the arms out and downward. At the bottom of the arc, cross the arms at the wrists again and shift your weight to the right foot. Bring the crossed arms up again in front of the body toward the head. At the head, they turn palms out and separate from one another. At the same time, bring the left knee up as you balance on the right leg.	Extend the left and right arms outward and kick slowly with the heel of the left leg at knee or hip level. The left hand should be lower than the right hand. The kick should be on the right rear diagonal. Although they are called "snap kicks," these kicks should be done very slowly in the 28-Step Form.

Movement 19: Left and Right Foot Snap Kick (continued)

19e	19f	19g	19h
As the left leg comes down, twist the foot outward to form a left twisting stance. At the same time, circle the hands downward as if scooping up energy from the earth.	Continue to circle the arms downward (as if scooping energy from the earth). Bend the knees. At the bottom of the arc, cross the arms at the wrists.	Bring the crossed arms up toward the head. At the head, turn the palms outward and circle the arms out and downward. At the bottom of the arc, cross the arms at the wrists again and shift your weight to the left foot. Bring the crossed arms up again in front of the body toward the head. At the head, they turn palms out and separate from one another. At the same time, bring the right knee up as you balance on the left leg.	Extend the left and right arms outward and kick slowly with the heel of the right leg at knee or hip level. The right hand should be lower than the left hand. The kick should be on the right front diagonal.

Movement 20: Left Heel Kick

Spiritual Name: One Good at Walking Leaves No Traces

| 20a | 20b | 20c |

After the previous kick, bring the right leg down with the toes pointing to the left front diagonal. As it touches the ground, shift your weight to it and form a cat stance facing the left. At the same time, raise the right arm overhead while the left hand is palm up by the waist.

Raise the left knee in preparation for the kick and turn the left palm outward to protect the right side of the chest.

Kick with the heel of the left foot while extending the left arm. The kick should be to the left. At the same time, extend the right hand up and the left hand down. Note that the centerline of the body is oriented to the front left diagonal, but the kick is to the left.

Movement 21: Twist One Step

Spiritual Name: To be Brave is to be Kind

21a

Bring the left foot down and turn it out to form a twist stance. Transfer your weight to the left leg and swing the arms in a horizontal arc toward the rear. The palms should be facing the rear.

21b

As the arms continue to swing past the body, step up with the right foot to form a half step stance.

Movement 22: Left Hand on Wrist

Spiritual Name: The Great Dwells in a Lowly Position

22a	22b	22c
Step out with the right foot. Turn the right hand palm up and form a fist and bring the left hand toward the right wrist.	With the left hand on the right wrist, swing both arms swing in a diagonal arc across the chest. At the same time, step out with the right foot to form a right twist stance.	As the right foot comes down to form a twist step, the toes are pointed to the left front diagonal, and the weight begins shifting to the right foot. The arms, with the left hand on the right wrist, swing just past the chest.

Movement 23: Move Block Fist

Spiritual Name: Within There is Essence

23a	**23b**	**23c**
From the previous position, step up with the left leg into a half-step stance. At the same time, leave the left hand with palm down in front of the body while retracting the right horizontal fist behind the body.	Step forward with the left leg to form a front stance facing the left. At the same time, punch forward with a right vertical fist while bringing the left hand toward the top of the right wrist.	Continue to transfer your weight forward to the left leg while punching forward with the right hand. Bring the left hand (palm down) to contact the right wrist.

Movement 24: Withdraw and Push

Spiritual Name: Knowing When to Stop is to be Safe

24a	24b	24c	24d
At the completion of the previous position, rock your weight forward to the left foot while lifting the right heel. At the same time, bring the left hand (palm down) under the right elbow.	Shift your weight to the rear leg to form a cat stance. At the same time, bring the left arm past the right elbow (turning the left hand palm up) and then past the right wrist. Separate the hands horizontally to each side as if forming a large horizontal circle.	Continue circling the hands back toward the body until they are in front of the chest with palms out.	Step forward with the left leg to form a bow stance. At the same time, push out with the hands.

Movement 25: Single Whip

Spiritual Name: Exposition of the Heavenly Mystery (Yin within Yang)

25a	25b	25c

From the previous position, shift your weight back to the right foot and bring the left foot back to form a half-step stance. At the same time, form a crane's beak with the right hand and bring the left palm close to it.

Step out with the left leg to form a bow stance facing the left. At the same time, bring your left hand toward the left.

Shift your weight to the left leg to complete the bow stance. At the same time, bring the left hand in front of the chest finishing with the left palm facing the front.

Movement 26: Cloud Hands (Stationary – 3x)

Spiritual Name: Move Without Exhaustion

| 26a | 26b | 26c |

From the left bow stance, rotate the rear foot to the front and then transfer your weight to it. Then bring the left foot up into a horse stance facing the front. At the same time, the right hand should open with the palm facing downward. The left hand should circle toward the lower tan tien with the palm up.

While in the horse stance, turn your body to the right front diagonal as you circle the right hand up and outward at shoulder level to the right with palm down. The elbow should be lower than the wrist. At the same time, your left hand, palm up at the lower tan tien, should follow the turn of the body to the right. Both hands should now be positioned as if holding a "ball" of energy. Shift your weight 60% to the right foot.

Turn your body to the left front diagonal as you circle the left hand up and outward at shoulder level to the left with palm down. The elbow should be lower than the wrist. At the same time, turn your right hand palm up and bring it to the lower tan tien level. Shift your weight 60% to the left foot. Repeat b & c two more times.

Movement 27: Cross Hands

Spiritual Name: Always Embrace the Source

| 27a | 27b | 27c |

From the last cloud hands position, while the left hand is still up, bring the right arm up to the left and then separate them as you circle them outward to the sides and then downward.

As you circle the arms downward, bend the knees. The motion of the hands are as if one is scooping energy from the earth. Keep the back straight. At the bottom of the circle, cross the hands (left over right) at the wrists.

Bring the crossed hands up in front of the middle tan tien (heart level). Palms should face the sides.

Movement 28: Completion of Tai Chi

Spiritual Name: Return to the Root

28a	28b	28c	28d
From the cross hands position, uncross the hands and let them descend in front of the body toward the thighs.	Turn the hands palms up and circle them out and toward the front, with elbows bent, to the level of the shoulders.	Let the hands descend slowly in front of the body toward the thighs.	Once the hands are at the thighs, the knees are still bent.

Movement 0: Wu Chi

Spiritual Name: The Great Void

0

Now let the hands move to the sides and straighten the knees. The ending stance is the same as the beginning stance. The form ends where it begins. This embodies the principle that the manifested energy (yin and yang) of the Tao ultimately returns to the creative stillness of Wu Chi – the unmanifested subtle essence of the Tao.

Closing Movement

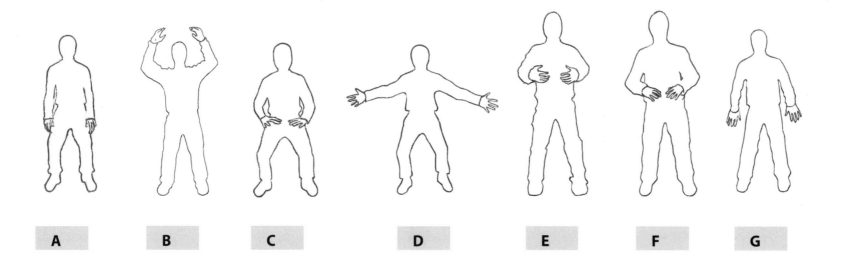

| A | B | C | D | E | F | G |

When Tai Chi practice is finished, it is important to perform a closing movement in order to draw the expanded energy (generated during Tai Chi practice) back down into the lower tan tien for storage. This can be done in a horse stance with knees slightly bent and arms down at the sides (Fig. A). Slowly circle the arms outward and upward. When they reach the overhead position, palms should be facing downward (Fig. B). Slowly let the arms descend (palms down) in front of the body toward the lower tan tien (Fig. C). When they reach the sides, circle the arms horizontally outward and toward the front at the level of the lower tan tien (Fig. D). When the arms reach the front, palms should be facing toward the body. Then slowly bring the hands toward the lower tan tien. Stop when the palms are about 12 inches from the lower tan tien. Remain in this position for a few minutes (Fig. E). This is the Tai Chi standing meditation position. Then turn the palms downward (Fig F) and let the arms descend to the sides as the knees straighten and the feet come together (Fig. G).

BREATHING: As the arms circle outward and upward, inhale. As they descend, exhale. As the arms circle horizontally outward and toward the front, inhale. As they are drawn toward the lower tan tien, exhale. All other times, breathe deeply and naturally.

19 Harmony Tai Chi - Long Form

Harmony Tai Chi is unique in that embodies the dynamics of styles such as the Yang, Chen, and Wu styles. Yet, in terms of energy cultivation, it focuses, not on a single energy center (e.g., the lower tan tien), but on balancing the energy of all three tan tien (lower, middle, and upper). As a complete method of self-cultivation, it can strengthen jing (essence), cultivate qi (energy), and refine or purify Shen (spirit). These three forms of energy are known as the "Three Treasures." It is the emphasis on the development of these Three Treasures that gives the Harmony Style its other name - "Trinity Style Tai Chi."

108 Posture Long Form

(Section designations follow the Tai Chi Chuan – Style of Harmony DVD)

Part I – Yin Section Postures

Common Names	Spiritual Names
Section A	
0. Wu Chi	The Great Void
1. Beginning Tai Chi	Existence before Heaven and Earth
2. Grasp the Sparrow's Tail	Gate of Subtle Origin
a. Brush Sleeve - R	Raise the Lower
b. Roll Back	Lower the Elevated
c. Press	Decrease the Overabundant
d. Push	Nourish the Insufficient

3.	Double Whip	The Exposition of Heavenly Mystery
		(Yang Within Yin)
4.	Lifting Hands - L&R	The Great Straightness Seems Crooked
5.	Hidden Tiger - R	To Give More is to Have More
6.	White Crane Spreads Its Wings (3x)	The Great Fullness Seems Empty
7.	Brush Knee – R	Empty and Yet Productive
8.	Playing the Lute – R	The Greatly Skilled Seems Clumsy
9.	Twist Step, Brush Knee – L	Empty and Yet Productive
10.	Playing the Lute – L	The Greatly Skilled Seems Clumsy
11.	Strike Forward Hands and Foot	The High and Low Assists Each Other
12.	Twist One Step Fist	To Be Brave is to Be Kind (One Step)
13.	Move Block Fist – L	Within There is Essence
14.	Withdraw and Push	Knowing When to Stop is to be Safe
15.	Cross Hands	Always Embrace the Source

Section B

16.	Embrace Tiger/Return to Mountain	To be Hollow is to be Filled
17.	Brush Knee – R & L	Empty Yet Productive
18.	Grasp the Sparrow's Tail	The Gate of Subtle Origin
	a. Roll Back	Lower the Elevated
	b. Press	Decrease the Overabundant
	c. Push	Nourish the Insufficient
19.	Oblique Double Whip	Exposition of the Heavenly Mystery
		(Yang Within Yin)
20.	Elbow Strike – L	To be Pliant is to be Whole
21.	Fist Under Elbow – R	To be Curled is to be Straight

22.	Repulse the Monkey (stationary - 4x, retreating-3x)	To Progress in Tao Seems Like Regressing
23.	Stir the Whirlpool	Draw from the Inexhaustible Source
24.	Searching for the Needle at Sea Bottom	The Feminine Yin can Overcome the Masculine Yang
25.	Diagonal Flying/Cross Hands in Twist	Straight but not Offensive Stance

Section C

26.	Block & Strike – L & R	Accomplishment by Non-Action
27.	White Crane Spreads Its Wings (3x)	The Great Fullness Seems Empty
28.	Brush Knee – R	Empty Yet Productive
29.	Search for Needle at Sea Bottom	The Feminine Yin can Overcome the Masculine Yang
30.	Push the Mountain – R & L	The Weak Overcomes the Strong
31.	White Snake Flicking Its Tongue	Within there is Evidence
32.	Hammer Fist – R	Thunder is the Source of Awakening
33.	Twist One Step Fist	To be Brave is to be Kind
34.	Move Block Fist – R	Within there is Essence
35.	Withdraw and Push	Knowing When to Stop is to be Safe
36.	Double Whip	Exposition of the Heavenly Mystery (Yang Within Yin)
37.	Cloud Hands (stationary-4x, moving to right-3x)	Move without Exhaustion
38.	Double Whip	Exposition of the Heavenly Mystery (Yang Within Yin)
39.	Brush Right Palm	Discreet Like a Humble Guest
40.	Left and Right Foot Snap Kick	Fording the Stream at Early Spring
41.	Left Heel Kick	One Good at Walking Leaves no Tracks
42.	Jump Step Strike Downwards	Pacify by the Nameless Simplicity

Section D

43.	Turn Body and Strike Behind	To Keep Behind is to Keep Ahead
44.	Twist Two Step Fist	To be Brave is to be Kind
45.	Move Block Fist – L	Within There is Essence
46.	Step Up, Left Kick and Palm Strike	To Win Without Contention
47.	Strike the Tiger – R & L	Being and Non-Being Brings Forth Each Other
48.	Left Kick Hands Part	Wholeness of Virtue Produces Unconditional Mind
49.	Knee Thrust Forward	To be Soft is to be Truly Strong
50.	Strike to The Ears	The Gate of All Wonders
51.	Left Heel Kick	One Good at Walking Leaves no Tracks
52.	Stir the Whirlpool	Draw from the Inexhaustible Source
53.	Sweeping the Lotus with One Leg	The Calm is the Master of the Overactive
54.	Right Shin Kick, Strike to Throat in	The High and Low Assist Each Other Concert
55.	Twist One Step Fist	To be Brave is to be Kind
56.	Move Block Fist	Within There is Essence
57.	Withdraw and Push	Knowing When to Stop is to be Safe
58.	Cross Hands	Always Embrace the Source

Part II – Yang Section Postures

Section 1

(Beginning Tai Chi)		(Existence Before Heaven and Earth)
59.	Embrace Tiger/Return to Mountain	To be Hollow is to be Filled
60.	Brush Knee – L & R	Empty Yet Productive
61.	Grasp the Sparrow's Tail	The Gate of Subtle Origin

	a. Roll Back	Lower the Elevated
	b. Press	Decrease the Overabundant
	c. Push	Nourish the Insufficient
62.	Oblique Single Whip	Exposition of the Heavenly Mystery
		(Yin Within Yang)
63.	Part the Horse's Mane with Circling	The Most Virtuous is like Water
	Double-Arm Strikes	
	a. Low Brush Sleeve – R	He Takes the Lowest Position
	b. Double Forearm Strike – R	He Does Not Contend with Others
	c. Low Brush Sleeve – L	He Takes the Lowest Position
	d. Double Forearm Strike – L	He Does Not Contend with Others
	e. Low Brush Sleeve – R	He Takes the Lowest Position
	f. Double Forearm Strike – R	He Does Not Contend with Others
64.	Grasp the Sparrow's Tail	The Gate of Subtle Origin
	a. Brush Sleeve – L	Raise the Lower
	b. Brush Sleeve – R	Raise the Lower
	c. Roll Back	Lower the Elevated
	d. Press	Decrease the Overabundant
	e. Push	Nourish the Insufficient
65.	Single Whip	Exposition of the Heavenly Mystery
		(Yin Within Yang)

Section 2

66.	Fair Lady Works the Shuttles (Four Corners)	Be Subtle yet Persisting
67.	Grasp the Sparrow's Tail	The Gate of Subtle Origin
	a. Brush Sleeve – L	Raise the Lower

b.	Brush Sleeve – R	Raise the Lower
c.	Roll Back	Lower the Elevated
d.	Press	Decrease the Overabundant
e.	Push	Nourish the Insufficient
68.	Single Whip	Exposition of the Heavenly Mystery (Yin Within Yang)

Section 3

69.	Snake Creeps Down	Deeply Rooting
70.	Golden Rooster Stands on One Leg – L	Know the Yang but Keep to the Yin
71.	Needle at Sea Bottom & Snap Kick to Front – L & R	To Shrink is to Stretch Out
72.	Diagonal Flying/Cross Hands in Twist	Straight but not Offensive Stance
73.	Shoulder Strikes – R & L	The Soft Overcomes the Hard
74.	White Crane Spreads Its Wings (3x)	The Great Fullness Seems Empty
75.	Twist Step, Brush Knee – L	Empty Yet Productive

Section 4

76.	Search for Needle at Sea Bottom	The Feminine Yin can Overcome the Masculine Yang
77.	Push the Mountain – L & R	The Weak Overcomes the Strong
78.	Left Hand on Wrist	The Great Dwells in a Lowly Position
79.	Right Hand on Wrist	The Great Dwells in a Lowly Position
80.	Move Block Fist – L	Within There is Essence
81.	Withdraw and Push	Knowing When to Stop is to be Safe
82.	Single Whip	Exposition of the Heavenly Mystery (Yin Within Yang)

83.	Cloud Hands (stationary-4x, to left-3x)	Move without Exhaustion
84.	Single Whip	Exposition of the Heavenly Mystery
		(Yin Within Yang)

Section 5

85.	High Pat on Horse	The Long and Short Form Each Other
86.	Cross-leg Kick – L	Journey of a Thousand Miles Begins With a Single Step
87.	White Snake Flicks Its Tongue	Within There is Evidence
88.	Turn Right Circle Kick	The Front and Rear Follow One Another
89.	Jump Step Downward Strike	Pacify by the Nameless Simplicity
90.	Stir the Cauldron (3x)	Life is Continually Renewing Itself
91.	Grasp the Sparrow's Tail	The Gate of Subtle Origin
	a. Brush Sleeve – R	Raise the Lower
	b. Roll Back	Lower the Elevated
	c. Press	Decrease the Overabundant
	d. Push	Nourish the Insufficient
92.	Single Whip	Exposition of the Heavenly Mystery
		(Yin Within Yang)

Section 6

93.	Cloud Hands (stationary, 4x)	Move without Exhaustion
94.	Double Low Cloud Hands (to the left, 3x)	There is no Climax to One's Extension and Expansion
95.	Single Whip	Exposition of the Heavenly Mystery
		(Yin Within Yang)
96.	Snake Creeps Down	Deeply Rooting
97.	Step Up to Form Seven Stars	Act Without Assertiveness
98.	Ride the Tiger Retreating	Retreat after Accomplishment

99.	White Crane Spreads its Wings	The Great Fullness Seems Empty

Section 7

100.	Stir the Whirlpool	Draw from the Inexhaustible Source
101.	Sweep the Lotus with One Leg	The Calm is the Master of the Overactive
102.	Right Circle Kick	The Front and Rear Follow One Another
103.	Shoot Tiger with Bow	The Truly Strong is the One Who Conquers Himself
104.	Twist Two Step Fist	To be Brave is to be Kind
105.	Move Block Fist	Within there is Essence
106.	Withdraw and Push	Knowing When to Stop is to be Safe
107.	Cross Hands	Always Embrace the Source
108.	Completion of Tai Chi	Return to the Root
0.	Wu Chi	The Great Void

20 Gentle Path Tai Chi

The three tan tien in the body are energy centers that also represent the three spheres of the human—body, mind and spirit or in Taoist terminology, essence (jing), energy (qi) and spirit (Shen). Gentle Path Tai Chi focuses on developing the lower tan tien which corresponds to essence. Functions such as growth, development, reproduction, and physical structure and vitality are all attributes of having abundance of essence. Without sufficient essence a person is likened to a broken vessel, unable to safely cross the turbulent waters of life for essence is also responsible for longevity and physical health. Consequently, the movements of Gentle Path tend to be lower, developing the legs, hips and lower torso.

88 Posture Form

Section I (Sections 1 and 2 on *Gentle Path Tai Chi* DVD)

1. Dragon Sharpening Its Claw
2. Dragon Flying Through the Sky
3. Independent Pine Tree/Sea Waves
4. Crane Exercising Its Wings
5. Eagle Searching Over the Ground
6. Crane Displaying Its Wings
7. Eagle Searching Over the Ground
8. Crane Displaying Its Wings
9. Southern Cross Moving on its Way
10. Immortal Peach under the Immortal Tree

11. Twin Trees of Yin and Yang

    (Cross Hands)

Section II (Sections 3 and 4 on *Gentle Path Tai Chi* DVD)

12. Immortal Pointing the Way

13. Wild Horse Turning Around

14. Big Windmill

15. Flying Dragon Circulating Its Wings

16. Great Archer Pulling His Bow

17. Turning the Disk of the Sky

18. Dragon Diving in the Deep Sea

19. Dragon Rising to the Heights

    (Cross Hands)

Section III (Sections 5 and 6 on *Gentle Path Tai Chi* DVD)

20. Dragon Moving Around in the Sky

21. Eagle Searching Over the Ground

22. Crane Arching Its Wings

23. Crane Circling in the Sky

24. Crane Twisting its Wings

25. Sun Meeting the Moon

26. Crane Twisting Its Wings

27. Sun Meeting the Moon

28. Immortal Peach Under the Immortal Tree

29. Twin Trees of Yin and Yang

    (Cross Hands)

Section IV (Section 7 and 8 on *Gentle Path Tai Chi* DVD)

30. Dragon Flying Through the Sky

31. Dragon Swinging Its Tail

32. Immortal Pointing the Way

33. Phoenix Landing on the Immortal Tree

34. Crane Flying High and Touching the Sky

35. Phoenix Landing on the Immortal Tree

36. Crane Flying High and Touching the Sky
    (Cross Hands)

Section V (Section 9 and 10 on *Gentle Path Tai Chi* DVD)

37. Light Crane Stepping Out

38. Seabird Taking Fish from the Ocean

39. Immortal Planting the Evergreen Tree

40. Rainbow Crossing the Sky

41. Twin Immortal Peaches

Section VI (Section 11 and 12 on *Gentle Path Tai Chi* DVD)

42. Climbing the Clouds

43. Great Archer Pulling His Bow

Section VII (Section 13 and 14 on *Gentle Path Tai Chi* DVD)

44. Shooting Star Chasing the Moon

45. Crane Landing on the Heavenly Pond

46. Crane Drinking from the Heavenly Pond

47. Crane Landing on the Heavenly Pond

48. Crane Drinking from the Heavenly Pond

49. Crane Gathering Back Its Leg

50. Embracing the Red Sun

Section VIII (Section 15 on the *Gentle Path Tai Chi* DVD)

51. Immortal Pointing the Way

52. Wild Horse Turning Around

53. Flying Horse Walking on the Clouds

54. Mighty Child Taming the Wild Horse

55. Gentle Tornado

56. Willow Dancing in the Gentle Breeze

57. Dragon Moving Around in the Sky

58. Eagle Searching Over the Ground

59. Crane Arching His Wings

60. Crane Circling in the Sky

61. Crane Twisting His Wings

62. Sun Meeting the Moon

63. Crane Twisting His Wings

64. Sun Meeting the Moon

65. Immortal Peach Under the Immortal Tree

66. Twin Trees of Yin and Yang

Section IX (Section 16 on the *Gentle Path Tai Chi* DVD)

67. Dragon Flying Through the Sky

68. Rising Tide Beating the Rocky Shore

69. Hawk Rising Up to the Sky

70. Ceiling of the Immortal Tree

71. Hawk Rising Up to the Sky

72. Fording Crane Looking at the Ground

73. Hurricane Sweeping Across the Ocean

74. Jade Girl Taming the Tiger

75. Twin Trees of Yin and Yang

Section X (Section 17 on the *Gentle Path Tai Chi* DVD)

76. Dragon Flying Through the Sky

77. Crane Piercing Through the Clouds

78. Phoenix Drinking from the Heavenly Lake

Section XI (Section 18 on the *Gentle Path Tai Chi* DVD)

79. Tornado Sweeping Over the Ground

80. Hurricane Crossing the Ocean

81. Eagle Riding on the Wind

82. Tornado Sweeping Over the Ground

83. Hurricane Crossing the Ocean

84. Eagle Riding on the Wind

85. Happy Child Dancing with the Sun, Moon, and Stars

86. Immortal Peach under the Immortal Tree

87. Twin Trees of Yin and Yang

88. Collecting the Energy (in the Lower Tan Tien)

21 Sky Journey Tai Chi

The middle tan tien is the resident of the Mind and the distribution center of energy or ai. Sky Journey is a bridge between the body and spirit, between Heaven and Earth and its chief purpose is the taming and cultivating of the mind and gathering of qi. Having undisturbed mind and abundance of energy are essential to actualizing one's life. Consequently, Sky Journey's movements tend to develop the middle, upper torso and arms and its speed is neither fast nor slow. The purpose of this chapter is to document the movements of this rare form of Tai Chi. The Sky Journey Tai Chi form can be seen in the *Tai Chi Chuan: An Appreciation* DVD by Hua Ching Ni. Please note that some of the movement names, which originally referred to Chinese astronomical constellations and phenomena, have been westernized to make it easier for a western audience to understand and appreciate.

85 Posture Form

Section I

1. Infinity Stance
2. A Star is Born – R
3. The Big Dipper Renews Its Cycle – R
4. Aurora Borealis Shimmers in the Sky
5. Haley's Comet Travels Toward the Sun – R
6. Virgo Combs Her Hair – R
7. The Moon Moves Across the Sky – L

Section II

8. A Star is Born – L

9. The Big Dipper Renews Its Cycle – L

10. Aurora Borealis Shimmers in the Sky

11. Looking at the Pole Star – L

12. Draco Follows the Big Dipper – R

13. Draco Follows the Big Dippler – L

14. Mighty Hercules Strikes – R

15. A Star is Born – R

Section III

16. Andromeda Breaks Her Chains

17. Centaurs Moves Higher in the Sky

18. The Shooting Star Chases the Moon – R

19. Bootes, the Herdsman, Stands Alert

20. Sagittarius Shoots His Bow – L

21. Sagittarius Shoots His Bow – R

22. Sagittarius Shoots His Bow – L

23. Scorpio Shows His Tail – L

24. Scorpio Shows His Tail – R

Section IV

25. The Horse Head Nebula – R

26. Mighty Hercules Strikes to the West

27. Virgo Combs Her Hair – R

28. The Moon Moves Across the Sky – L

29. Leo the Lion Opens His Giant Mouth – R

30. Leo the Lion Opens His Giant Mouth – L

31. Leo the Lion Opens His Giant Mouth – R

Section V

32. Libra Balances Her Scales

33. The Immortal Points the Way – R

34. The Thunder Roars – R

35. The Thunder Roars – L

36. The Spiraling Nebula

37. Expanding Orion – L

38. Cancer the Crab Moves on His Way – L

39. Thunder in the East

40. The Active Gemini Twins Descend

Section VI

41. Cygnus the Swan Ascends

42. The Spiraling Nebula

43. Expanding Orion

Section VII

44. Cancer the Crab Moves on His Way – R

45. The Auspicious Trine of Three Stars

46. Virgo Combs Her Hair – L

47. The Moon Moves Across the Sky – R

48. Young Taurus Scratches His Horns – R

49. Young Taurus Scratches His Horns – L

50. Aquarius Pours the Water

51. Thunder in the East

52. Virgo Combs Her Hair – R

53. The Moon Moves Across the Sky – L

Section VIII

54. Cassiopeia's Dance Step

55. Thunder in the East

56. The Weaving Maiden (Vega) Works Her Shuttle

57. Moving Clouds – R

58. Thunder Roars Twice in the South

59. Happy Pisces Jumps into the Air – L

60. Happy Pisces Jumps into the Air – R

61. Sagittarius Shoots His Bow – R

62. Sagittarius Shoots His Bow – L

63. Sagittarius Shoots His Bow – R

Section IX

64. Scorpio Shows His Tail – R

65. Scorpio Shows His Tail – L

66. The Horse Head Nebula – L

67. Mighty Hercules Strikes – L

68. Virgo Combs Her Hair – L

Section X

69. The Moon Travels Across the Sky – R

70. Leo the Lion Opens His Giant Mouth – R, L, R

22 Infinite Expansion Tai Chi

The upper tan tien is the spirit center of the body, the consciousness of our being and the connection to the Universal Divine Source. By cultivating and developing the upper tan tien through Infinite Expansion Tai Chi, a student can experience the unlimited potential of human spiritual growth. Infinite Expansion movements focus on the upper body in a spiral upward motion to the top of the head where hundreds of spirits gather. The mastery of Infinite Expansion brings the individual closer to oneness with the Universal Essence. The purpose of this chapter is to document the movements of the Infinite Expansion Tai Chi form. This rare form of Tai Chi can be seen in the *Tai Chi Chuan: An Appreciation* DVD by Hua Ching Ni.

67 Posture Form

Section I

1. Union of Heaven & Earth
2. Crashing the Boundless – R
3. Bringing All into Harmony – R
4. Taming the Flying Dragon of Impulse – L
5. Crashing the Boundless – R
6. Delight in Peace
7. Riding on the Light
8. Quieting the Restless Monkey Mind
9. Revelation of the Indivisible
10. A Stride Covering All Time and Space
11. The Meeting of Yin and Yang

12. Sublimating the Impure

13. Reconciling with the Contrary

14. Roaming the Realm of No Limit – L, R, L

15. Riding the Time Tunnel Backwards – L, R, L

16. Delight in Peace

17. Riding the Light

18. Flowing with Nature

19. Breaking All Boundaries

20. Riding the Whirlwind of No Confrontation

21. Blending the Myriad Things Back to Oneness

22. Revitalizing Heaven and Earth

23. Extending the Unobstructed Spirit

24. Finding Pleasure Beyond the Dust of the World – L, R, L

25. Mounting the Height of No Haughtiness

26. Great Eloquence Needs No Words

27. Triumph Over the High and Low

28. Reaching the Non-Above

29. Wandering with Perfect Freedom

30. Excursion into the Infinite

Section II

31. Uniting with the Non-Being of the Subtle Origin

32. Bringing All into Harmony

33. Taming the Flying Dragon of Impulse

34. The Universe is Covered in One Step

35. Moving with the Rhythm of the Mother's Breath

36. Untying All Entanglements – R, L, R

37. Traveling Back to Unity

38. Smoothing All into Oneness

39. Flying with No Wind

40. Clearing the Sky & Emotions

41. Plunging to the Depths and Spiraling to the Heights – R

42. Plunging to the Depths and Spiraling to the Heights – L

Section III

43. Riding the Time Tunnel Backwards – L, R, L

44. Delight in Peace

45. Riding the Light

46. Flowing with Nature

47. Breaking All Boundaries

48. Riding the Whirlwind of No Confrontation

49. Blending the Myriad Things Back to Oneness (3x)

50. Revitalizing Heaven and Earth – L, R, L

51. Extending the Unobstructed Spirit – R

52. Riding the Wings of Yin and Yang

53. Subduing the Demon of Too Much Desire

54. Crashing the Boundless

55. Bringing All into Harmony

56. Flowing with Nature

57. Befriending the Absolute

58. Carrying the Sun & Moon Across the Galaxy

59. Subduing the Demon

60. Crashing the Boundless – L

61. Bringing All into Harmony – L

62. Taming the Flying Dragon of Impulse – R

63. Carrying the Sky on Your Back

64. Turning to Gather All Back to the Source

65. Touching the Peak of No Peak

66. Crashing Through the Boundless

67. Returning to Unite Heaven and Earth

23 Tai Chi Instrument Forms

The Ni Family Tradition of Tai Chi includes a number of esoteric forms using various instruments (traditional weapons). These include forms for single straight sword, broadsword, staff, Tai Chi fan, Tai Chi ruler, and Tai Chi ball. These Tai Chi instrument forms are used for spiritual cultivation and concentration. There is no "enemy" except for the negative and destructive energies and blockages within ourselves. These forms can be used to cultivate virtue and break through negative energy blockages. The postures for these various forms are too numerous to document here. However, those for the Tai Chi single straight sword long form are given below.

Single Straight Sword Long Form - 33 Postures

Common Names	Spiritual Names
1. Commence form	Tai Chi divides
2. Looking at the sword tip	Manifesting heaven and earth
3. Turning overhead block & cradle the sword	Clarity of the mind assists the universal heart
4. Back sweeping cut	Great awakening makes one strong
5. Frontal upward slice	The subtle light removes all darkness
6. Back cut while standing on one leg	All obstacles are cleared away beneath
7. Side upper right block	Embrace the subtle vibration from the great light
8. Front downward cut	The power of universal love protects all lives
9. Retract the sword, point sword hand forward	A mind that is peaceful allows no negativity
10. Twist step and downward thrust	Great success is accomplished bit by bit
11. Plant the sword	Be rooted in your natural virtue

12. Untwist & straight forward thrust	A settled mind is a free mind
13. Twist step, look back, step and thrust to throat	A good world starts with your refinement
14. Retract & turn, side thrust to ribs	Troubles breed emotion, emotion leads to trouble
15. Plant the sword	Be rooted in your natural virtue
16. Retract the sword while standing on one leg	The power of universal heart protects all things
17. Three upward circular cuts while advancing	Its easy to be lost in a whirlwind existence
18. Retract the sword & crouch	Gather your essence and be like the water
19. Lunge and thrust forward	The truth of life comes from deep spiritual understanding
20. Retract the sword & stand ready	Quietude engenders profound realization
21. Lunge forward & thrust while squatting	The wisdom of deep penetration reveals the way
22. Retreat & lean backwards	Before extension, there is contraction
23. Backward circular strike	When the heart clears no obstacle can remain
24. Forward handle strike	One of spiritual dignity is not afraid of being in the dark
25. Back cut while standing on one leg	A nebulous mind produces suffering
26. Overhead sword block	The power of goodness engenders wisdom
27. Sweep and twirl blocks	Deep enlightenment reaches no self
28. Turn, sit, and thrust under arm	The way is attained by not holding onto any expectation
29. Twisting overhead block	Intellectual intent and meddling bring trouble
30. Sword behind back, point sword hand forward	The heart of the integral way is the heart of peace
31. Splitting strike to side standing on one leg	To practice purity and sincerity, one must cleanse all improper desires
32. Retract and thrust to side	With great concentration one becomes truthful and pure
33. Circle overhead & return to the origin	Return to the origin of pre-heaven and the infinite

Conclusion

You have an opportunity for success with Tai Chi movement and Qigong. One important element that can truly serve you is to have great confidence in what you have chosen to do by practicing it constantly. With practice and perseverance, you shall achieve your goals. Many people have attained a long and happy life, and we wish the same for you.

The most essential teaching of the Integral Way is the knowledge of how to move internal power outwardly for a positive purpose. Practically, it is a training in fearlessness and healthy self-confidence. The most essential practice is to become "the one of universal self-responding truth within all people." Quite simply, it is the sound of "Hon!" (thunder). This means to ignore complications and just go ahead with your upright life!

Now that you have finished reading the book, the real fun is just begun. You have an opportunity to turn what you learn from Tai Chi into healthy self-confidence and fearlessness in your life. The consistent and determined practice of Tai Chi will bring you far more emotional and spiritual joy than only doing things like reading books and watching television. Eventually, you will discover and experience the profound "secrets" of the Universe unfolding within this simple and yet powerful cosmic dance. We invite you to tune in and start moving your life to the music of the primordial beat today and enliven your mind, body and spirit.

Footnotes

Chapter 1

1. The word "shen" can refer to two aspects of spiritual energy. When we use "shen" with a lowercase "s", it refers to the subtle spiritual energy associated with the heart. When we use "Shen" with an uppercase "S", it refers in general to all of the subtle spirits or spiritual energies of the body (e.g., the shen, po, hun, I, and chih).

2. These steps of taoist internal alchemy have the smaller goal of health and longevity and the larger goal of spiritual immortality. For further discussion, see *Internal Alchemy* and *Workbook for Spiritual Development*.

3. see the *Complete Works of Lao Tzu*.

Chapter 3

1. see *Attune Your Body with Dao-In* book and DVD

2. see *The Eight Treasures* book and DVD

3. see *The Complete Works of Lao Tzu*

Chapter 4

1. see *Tao: The Subtle Universal Law and the Integral Way of Life*, Chapter 2

2. see *The Complete Works of Lao Tzu* (*Tao Te Ching*, Chapter 55)

3. see *The Golden Message*, Part I; or visit www.integralway.org for more information about the Integral Way

4. see *Nuture Your Spirits*

Chapter 5

1. see *Cosmic Tour Ba Gua* DVD

2. see *I Ching, The Book of Changes and the Unchanging Truth*

3. see *Life & Teaching of Two Immortals, Volume II: Chen Tuan*, p. 73-74

Chapter 6

1. see *The Complete Works of Lao Tzu* (*Hua Hu Ching*, Chapter 39, p. 150)

Chapter 7

1. see *The Complete Works of Lao Tzu* (*Tao Te Ching*, Chapter 42, p. 60)

2. These are the spiritual subtle energies associated with the 5 major organ systems of traditional Chinese medicine. The correspondences are as follows: shen (heart), po (lungs), hun (liver), I (spleen), and chih (kidneys). In Taoist terminology, these are referred to as the body's "spirits." For a further discussion of this, see *Nuture Your Spirits*.

Chapter 9

1. quoted from *The Esoteric Tao Teh Ching*, Chapter 30, p. 60.

2. see *Internal Alchemy*.

Chapter 10

1. see *Attune Your Body with Dao-In* book and DVD.

2. e.g., see *I Ching, The Book of Changes and the Unchanging Truth*

3. e.g., see *The Complete Works of Lao Tzu*

4. see *Workbook for Spiritual Development*

5. see *The Eight Treasures: Energy Enhancement Exercise*

Chapter 11

1. see *The Eight Treasures: Energy Enhancement Exercise*

2. The three spheres are Tai Ching, Shan Ching, and Yu Ching – see *The Complete Works of Lao Tzu*, p. 196-200 for further explanation.

Chapter 13

1. see *Tai Chi Chuan: Style of Harmony* DVD.

2. To observe Gentle Path Tai Chi, see Master Hua-Ching Ni's DVD, *Tai Chi Chuan: The Gentle Path*

3. To observe Sky Journey Tai Chi, see Master Hua Ching Ni's DVD, *Tai Chi Chuan: An Appreciation.*

4. To observe Infinite Expansion Tai Chi, see Master Hua Ching Ni's DVD, *Tai Chi Chuan: An Appreciation.*

Chapter 14

1. see *The Eight Treasures Energy Enhancement Exercise.*

Chapter 15

1. see *The Eight Treasures Energy Enhancement Exercise* book and DVD.

Bibliography

Chan K, Qin L, Lau M, Woo J, Au S, Choy W, Lee K, Lee S (2004) A randomized, prospective study of the effects of Tai Chi Chuan exercise on bone mineral density in postmenopausal women. *Arch Phys Med Rehabil.* 85:717-722.

Chao YF, Chen SY, Lan C, Lai JS (2002) The cardiorespiratory response and energy expenditures of Tai Chi Qui Gong. *Am J Chin Med.* 30:451-461.

Christou EA, Yang Y, Rosengren KS (2003) Taiji training improves knee extensor strength and force control in older adults. *J Gerontol A Biol Sci Med Sci.* 58:763-766.

Irwin MR, Pike JL, Cole JC, Oxman MN (2003) Effects of a behavioral intervention, Tai Chi Chih, on varicella-zoster virus specific immunity and health functioning in older adults. *Psychosom Med.* 65:824-830.

Lan C, Chen SY, Lai JS, Wong MK (2001) Heart rate responses and oxygen consumption during Tai Chi practice. *Am J Chin Med.* 29:403-410.

Li F, Fisher KJ, Harmer P, McAuley E (2002) Delineating the impact of Tai Chi training on physical function among the elderly. *Am J Prev Med.* 23:92-97

Li F, Fisher KJ, Harmer P, Irbe D, Tearse RG, Weimer C (2004) Tai Chi and self-rated quality of sleep and daytime sleepiness in older adults: a randomized controlled trial. *J Am Geriatr Soc.* 52:892-900.

Li F, Harmer P, McAuley E, Duncan TE, Duncan SC, Chaumeton N, Fisher KJ (2001) An evaluation of the effects of Tai Chi exercise on physical function among older persons: a randomized controlled trial. *Ann Behav Med.* 23:139-146.

Li JX, Hong Y, Chan KM (2001) Tai Chi: physiological characteristics and beneficial effects on health. *Br J Sports Med.* 35:148-156.

Liu Y, Mimura K, Wang L, Ikuda K (2003) Physiological benefits of 24-style Taijiquan exercise in middle-aged women. *J Physiol Anthrool Appl Human Sci.* 22:219-225.

Lu WA, Kuo CD (2003) The effect of Tai Chi Chuan on the autonomic nervous modulation in older persons. *Med Sci Sports Exerc.* 35:1972-1976.

Qin L, Au S, Choy W, Leung P, Neff M, Lee K, Lau M, Woo J, Chan K (2002) Regular Tai Chi Chuan exercise may retard bone loss in postmenopausal women: a case-control study. *Arch Phys Med Rehabil.* 83:1355-1359.

Schaller K (1996) Tai Chi Chih: an exercise option for older adults. *J Gerontol Nurs.* 22:12-17.

Song R, Lee EO, Lam P, Bae SC (2003) Effects of Tai Chi exercise on pain, balance, muscle strength, and perceived difficulties in physical functioning in older women with osteoarthritis: a randomized clinical trial. *Journal of Rheumatology,* 30, 2039-2044.

Taggart HM (2002) Effects of Tai Chi exercise on balance, functional mobility, and fear of falling among older women. *Appl Nurs Res.* 15:235-242.

Taggart HM, Arslanian CL, Bae S, Singh K (2003) Effects of Tai Chi exercise on fibromyalgia symptoms and health-related quality of life. *Orthop Nurs.* 22:353-360.

Taylor-Piliae RE (2003) Tai Chi as an adjunct to cardiac rehabilitation exercise training. *J Cardiopulm Rehabil.* 23:90-96.

Taylor-Piliae RE, Froelicher ES (2004) Effectiveness of Tai Chi exercise in improving aerobic capacity: a meta-analysis. *J Cardiovasc Nurs.* 19:48-57.

Thorton EW, Sykes KS, Tang WK (2004) Health benefits of Tai Chi exercise: improved balance and blood pressure in middle-aged women. *Health Prom Int.* 19:33-38.

Tsai JC, Wang WH, Chan P, Lin LJ, Wang CH, Tomlinson B, Hsieh MH, Yang HY, Liu JC (2003) The beneficial effects of Tai Chi Chuan on blood pressure and lipid profile and anxiety status in a randomized controlled trial. *J Altern Complement Med.* 9:747-754.

Tsang WW, Hui-Chan CW (2003) Effects of Tai Chi on joint proprioception and stability limits in elderly subjects. *Med Sci Sports Exerc.* 35:1962-1971.

Tsang WW, Hui-Chan CW (2004) Effects of exercise on joint sense and balance in elderly men: Tai Chi versus golf. *Med Sci Sports Exerc.* 36:658-667.

Tsang WW, Hui-Chan CW (2004) Effect of 4- and 8-wk intensive Tai Chi training on balance control in the elderly. *Med Sci Sports Exerc.* 36:648-657.

Tsang WW, Wong VS, Fu SN, Hui-Chan CW (2004) Tai Chi improves standing balance control under reduced or conflicting sensory conditions. *Arch Phys Med Rehabil.* 85:129-137.

Verhagen AP, Immink M, van der Meulen A, Bierma-Zeinstra SM (2004) The efficacy of Tai Chi Chuan in older adults: a systematic review. *Fam Pract.* 21:107-113.

Wang C, Collet JP, Lau J (2004) The effect of Tai Chi on health outcomes in patients with chronic conditions: a systematic review. *Arch Intern Med.* 164:493-501.

Wang JS, Lan C, Wong MK (2001) Tai Chi Chuan training to enhance microcirculatory function in healthy elderly men. Arch Phys Med Rehabil. 82:1176-1180.

Wang JS, Lan C, Chen SY, Wong MK (2002) Tai Chi Chuan training is associated with enhanced endothelium-dependent dilation in skin vasculature of healthy older men. *J Am Geriatr Soc.* 50:1024-1030.

Wayne PM, Krebs DE, Wolf SL, Gill-Body KM, Scarborough DM, McGibbon CA, Kaptchuk TJ, Parker SW (2004) Can Tai Chi improve vestibulopathic postural control? *Arch Phys Med Rehabil.* 85:142-152.

Wolf SL, Barnhart HX, Kutner NG, McNeely E, Coogler C, Xu T (1996) Reducing frailty and falls in older persons: an investigation of tai chi and computerized balance training. *J Am Geriatr Soc.* 44:489-497.

Wu G, Zhao F, Zhou X, Wei L (2002) Improvement of isokinetic knee extensor strength and reduction of postural sway in the elderly from long-term Tai Chi exercise. *Arch Phys Med Rehabil.* 83:1364-1369.

Xu D, Hong Y, Li J, Chan K (2004) Effect of Tai Chi exercise on proprioception of ankle and knee joints in old people. *Br J Sports Med.* 38:50-54.

Appendix

The following interview with Master Ni was originally published as an article in *Inside Kung Fu Magazine* in the May 1978 (vol. 5, no. 3) issue. In it, he does not discuss Tai Chi, the movement art, specifically but rather talks about Taoist principles and cosmology. The article is included here because understanding the Taoist view of the universe is an essential foundation for understanding the full importance of Tai Chi as a means of cultivating a healthy body, mind, and spirit.

Interview With Master Ni Hua-Ching

On Taoist Principles and Cosmology

(from *Inside Kung Fu Magazine*, May 1978, Vol 5, No. 3)

By Suzanne Soehner

Master Ni personally represents a direct and continuous lineage of 37 generations of Taoist tradition, dating back to the Tang Dynasty of China (677 A.D.). He is also the heir and embodiment of the wisdom and experience which has been transmitted in an unbroken succession for 74 generations, dating back to the Han Dynasty (216 B.C.).

As a young boy, he has chosen to study with Taoist Masters in the high mountains of mainland China. After more than 20 years of intensive training, he was fully acknowledged and empowered as a true master of all traditional Taoist disciplines, including Tai Chi Chuan, Kung Fu, meditation, acupuncture and herbal medicine. Master Ni has taught and practiced these arts on the island of Taiwan for 27 years and has written over 50 books on various Taoist subjects.

Because of the social changes which have taken place in China in recent history, Master Ni is the last in his lineage to be taught by ancient traditional methods, and is the only Taoist master with these credentials teaching in the United States. Until now, this knowledge has been almost unavailable outside of China.

Master Ni is presently here for a limited period of time to share his wisdom and experience with serious students who are willing to make the effort to cultivate and develop themselves to their fullest potential.

IKF: Would you tell us something about your own background and training?

MASTER NI: Traditionally, a Taoist does not like to talk about himself as a special individual existence. However, this is a special occasion. First, let us understand that traditionally, the esoteric knowledge of the ancient Chinese was transmitted through an apprentice system and through family continuation. I was born into one of those families with a Taoist heritage and with the responsibility to preserve this culture. Besides my father, who was my first traditional teacher, I had the special opportunity to learn from three other great masters who lived as hermits at that time in some very beautiful, high mountains. They passed their traditional knowledge and techniques to me, making me one spiritual descendant of this prehistoric tradition: the Union of Tao and Man. This mainstream of Taoism maintains that man was born with the Tao as his inherent, true nature. However, he loses and separates himself from the Tao in his worldly life. Thus out spiritual goal of life is to reunite ourselves with our true nature – the reunion of Tao and man. Or we may put it this way. Mankind was born in a very balanced state. However, after living in the world, desire outgrew intelligence, causing imbalance and creating disaster, misery and agony, taking us far away from our true nature. This is why we need the Taoist self-cultivation to reconstruct within ourselves the image of the "Shien" or Immortal – a being united in body, mind and spirit with nature. This is my simple background, as well as my tradition.

IKF: What is Taoism? How does it differ from other spiritual traditions?

MASTER NI: Firstly, I don't think it is appropriate to use "ism" to limit or try to title Tao. The reason is that when we talk about a kind of "ism" we are generally referring to some kind of political principle, economic policy, or special view of life. Tao cannot be referred to as products fashioned from it. The Taoist tradition constitutes one branch or school of world knowledge which has accumulated over thousands of years. The title of "Taoism" was used only to differentiate it from other traditions. You may say that Tao is the essence of the universe which is pre-heaven and pre-earth, existing before anything became formed. It is the unmanifest potentiality from which all manifestations proceed. After things become mentally or physically formed, they then are given names or titles. The names and titles are not the Tao but are its descriptions. This process can also be applied to describe our mind. When our mind is perfectly still and we have not yet formed it into any ideas, concepts, images or attitudes, it is the true Mind itself. This is so even if one is not aware of its existence. Actually, it is only when one is involved in something, excited or disturbed, that one is aware of the mind. Pure Mind in Taoist terms is called "Po". This may be translated as the original simplicity or the primary essence. It is sthe fundamental power of mind. When pure mental energy connects with the universal, unmanifest, creative energy, it is also called Po or Tao, the Original Simplicity. In its unmanifest aspect, the Original Simplicity is infinite. When it becomes manifest, it is finite.

Religions were originally created in human society out of mankind's mental need to understand and control its environment, as an expression of the evolution of human consciousness. Religions can take as many forms as man's mind may take. However, all theological inventions are of secondary importance and are not the original Po itself, which should not be molded or distorted in order to worship its accessories. Religion is the creation of the mind, and therefore, it relies upon psychological experience and intellectual discovery. Consequently, what religion is about is the worship of these experiences. But Taoism begins with the essential, intuitive understanding of the origin and nature of the universe. The quality of Taoism is different than that of worldly religions as Taoism doesn't emphasize worship. Worship is a secondary, mental activity. When you move your mind by creating the sentiment of worship, you fashion something outside of the mind as the object of your worship. By so doing, you trap your mind in the illusion of duality, which is against Tao. Rather than invent an outside sovereignty to act as his authority, the Taoist perceives the worshipper and the worshipped as one. When a Taoist engages in worship, by so doing he is revering the objectivization of his own true nature. Relatively speaking, the goal of Taoism is the reunification of oneself with the great Po, the primal, creative energy which is the essence of the universe. The highest, most refined energy within us is of the same frequency as the primal energy referred to as Po.

Your life is one hand of the primal energy of the universe extending itself outward as your Self. It is not like one fish which jumped out of the ocean. We are an extension of the universal power which has stretched itself outward, not only into humankind but into all manifestations. Since we have lost our Po, our Original Simplicity or original essence, in our habitual mental perception of duality and multiplicity, we need to restore ourselves back to the great creative, Original Simplicity. In Chinese the Original Simplicity is called "yuen chi", the original, beginning energy. With yuen chi we can do anything. If we disperse or scatter the yuen chi, we can do nothing. So the Original Simplicity is not a doctrine, it's the substance of all beings. The Taoist cultivates his energy in order to realize his true nature. The Taoist way is not merely a worship service or something like this. We just call it self-cultivation. As an aspect of self-cultivation, the Taoist tradition also includes the practice of certain rituals or formulas in order to bring about a response from the super-physical natural power. These are some of the activities and non-activities which comprise today's Taoism.

The Taoist tradition in China has, over many years, gradually divided into two main groups, and even many smaller branches. One group preserves the original spirit of Taoism, while the other pays more attention to ceremonies. I belong to the former, maintaining the original spirit of Taoism. My tradition is not connected with the local customs of different Chinese villages – the so-called Taoist folk religion.

QUESTION: Why have you come to America?

MASTER NI: I came to the United States at the invitation of some American students who came to Taiwan to study with me. After some time they invited me to come to this country. Before coming here I practiced traditional Chinese medicine on that island. I also taught Tai Chi Chuan and passed on Taoism. While I was in Taiwan I wrote many books on Taoism, with a wide readership interested in learning Taoism through me. The reason for my accepting the invitation to come here was based on my own understanding of today's world crisis. The decisive power of human destiny is mainly mankind itself. There is a very old Chinese proverb which says: "When nature makes difficulties, mankind still has the opportunity to avoid the problem and survive. But when man himself creates disaster, it is hard for him to run away." Today's international social conflicts are based mainly on the difference between an error in people's concept of God and the nature of life.

The Roman emperors were the first to understand that Christianity could be used as a good ruling tool. Since then, Christianity has played an important part in all of Western society. The root of the problem is that the true quality of Christianity is more sociological than spiritual. The foundation of present day Christianity is based on the shallow, emotional level of understanding. Today's church leaders emphasize emotional force such as faith, hope and love. But they use Christianity to blind the directing eye of reason. Thus, strong prejudice was nursed and was made a persecution force for the free soul. We all know that one's view of the universe influences his view of life. This view of life can influence a person's personality.

Besides Christianity and Christianity-type religions, what other view of the universe does Western society hold? One can look in a college astronomy textbook and find that there are two main theories of the beginning of the universe. One is that the universe had no beginning at all. What exists now is the same thing that has always existed. This is one theory. The second main theory is what is called the "Big Bang" theory, which states that there originally existed a "cosmic egg" of primordial energy and then there was a big explosion and many smaller galaxies resulted. This is the Western society's heritage and culture. From a Taoist perspective, the Big Bang theory presumes the existence of time and space prior to the creation of the universe, whereas the Taoist sees time and space as one of the developmental attributes of the universe. But I would rather discuss Taoist cosmology. I just mentioned this because the view one holds of the universe is so important in influencing one's activities and the whole of human society. Through Taoist cosmology one may know the universal law. You may call it Tao. Tao is the substance of the universe. As it extends, develops and evolves, yin and yang manifest as the Tai Chi principle, which then splits and becomes three levels of existence, manifesting as the spiritual, mental and physical planes. You might say as a way of physics, mind is the most sensitive energy, spirit is the most subtle, and physical energy is the grossest. The Taoist cosmology holds a peaceful and orderly view of the universe. Such a view can bring a peaceful mind and a creative attitude. You may also know that to connect yourself with the deep root of the universe, the highest subtlety, utilizes your calm mind, your high level energy, not the lower emotional energy. Emotion is mostly a product of your relative activity. It is not the deep mind of the absolute world. I came to America with the hope that through my teaching, people will be able to see a reasonable and integrated view of the universe. Through such reasonable understanding, the development of mankind's future will be bright. An individual life, with the foundation of understanding the origin and nature of the universe, can know that life does not finish at the end of the physical life. Life is connected with the whole universe. This understanding can help to eliminate the conflict in the world's thinking, the conflict that arises out of different, erroneous views of God and the nature of life. Generally, all religions are a kind of logic. If you follow an incorrect logic, you will arrive at an incorrect result. The religion and culture of a people are the manifestation of the mental energy of the people. If the correct logic is applied, the resulting manifestations will be harmonious.

IKF: What is the *I Ching*?

MASTER NI: The *I Ching* is the foundation of all Chinese intellectual systems. All eminent achievements of Chinese acupuncture, geomancy (the energy arrangements and relationships of one's environment), military philosophy and strategy, Chinese architecture, and so forth, are derived from the *I Ching*. The study of the *I Ching* has reaped an abundant harvest of knowledge throughout its long history, which dates back over 5,000 years. However, even a natural-born Chinese scholar still has difficulty comprehending its profound imminence. I, as heir to the heritage of the mainstream of Taoism, in order to create other Taoist spiritual heirs, choose and lead students to the profound secrets of the I Ching, which are the foundation upon which Taoism is developed.

Originally, the *Book of Changes* contained no written words at all. It only had signs made up of three or six lines, either broken, representing yin energy, or unbroken, representing yang energy. Originally, the signs were composed of three lines. All of the possible combinations of three yin and/or yang lines resulted in eight main signs known as the Pa Kua. As time passed, some later stages doubled the signs, making six lines, which had sixty-four possible combinations. These signs are a concrete indication of all the energy manifestations of the universe, how they are formed and how they function. The basic principles are the yin and yang, displaying duality. Yin and yang have many translations, such as the two sides of positive and negative, expansion and contraction, construction and destruction, masculine and feminine. Yin and yang are not two separate energies or activities. The activity of one is inherently contained within and created by the other. For example, a symphony is composed not only of musical sounds. The silent pauses between the sounds are also an intrinsic aspect of the composition. In the English language, the contradictory sense of positive and negative is strong. But in the Chinese way of thinking, the yin and yang may unite themselves, and through this union the existence of all things is made possible. If one side is excessive, its state of balance is lost, thereby creating the possibility of destruction. In Western thinking, positive and negative must fight each other on opposite sides. But the Chinese concept of yin and yang shows us that the great harmony of the universal development is based on the cooperation and union of apparent opposites. The *I Ching* shows that the universe is one whole, but with two wings, like man with two legs. In order to function effectively, the two legs don't fight each other, but they work together to help each other. For example, in movement, when you produce one kind of force to push yourself up and forward, at the same time you also produce a kind of rejecting force. This principle can be applied to everything, with yin and yang united as a Tai Chi. The Tai Chi then evolves into three levels of existence; physical existence, spiritual existence, and the combination of the two, which is mental existence. Human beings are one manifestation of mental existence, and are a good example of the unification of the physical and spiritual. Through the study of the *I Ching* one may come to know and experience the mysterious generating origin of the universe, achieve spiritual development and keep pace with the evolution of the universe.

IKF: Why do you teach the *I Ching* or *Book of Changes*?

MASTER NI: Some of my students have brought translations of the *I Ching* to me. It is very difficult to make a translation – especially since the Chinese mental structure is so different from that of Westerners. Even the most excellent of translators have trouble. So none of the translations are perfect. There are many mistakes and most of the translations are superficial. Only one who is born into this tradition has had his mind molded by it. With the added advantage of Taoist enlightenment training comes the development of high comprehension and familiarity with all of the historical aspects involved, thereby deepening the understanding of exactly what is meant in the *Book of Changes*. We do not have many translations here in America, but in China we have maybe a thousand famous books discussing it. However, one must have excellent training in order to distinguish the true information from the false. The reason I think the *Book of Changes* is worthy of teaching is that when one practices the *I Ching*, one can find external evidence showing the connection between oneself and the universal subtle energy – the melting of subjectivity and objectivity. This evidence can guide you and encourage you to move forward into the mysterious realms. Through the practice of the *I Ching* one may prove the possibility of uniting subjectivity and objectivity into one whole.

Resources

Books from the Ni Family

I Ching, The Book of Changes and the Unchanging Truth—This legendary classic is recognized as the first written book of wisdom. Leaders and sages throughout history have consulted it as a trusted advisor, which reveals the appropriate action in any circumstance. Includes over 200 pages of background material on natural energy cycles, instruction and commentaries.

#BBOOK—669 pages, hardcover. $35.00

Tao, the Subtle Universal Law—Most people are unaware that their thoughts and behavior evoke responses from the invisible net of universal energy. To lead a good stable life is to be aware of the universal subtle law in every moment of our lives. This book presents practical methods that have been successfully used for centuries to accomplish this.

#BTAOS—208 pages, softcover. $12.95

The Complete Works of Lao Tzu - Written around 500 B.C., the Tao Teh Ching is one of the most frequently translated and most cherished works in the world. The Complete Works of Lao Tzu by Master Ni is a remarkable elucidation of the famed Tao Teh Ching. It is the only known written record of Lao Tzu's orally transmitted teaching, the Hua Hu Ching. As the only book of Lao Tzu written by a Taoist Master in the English language, it is little wonder it remains one of our most popular books.

#BCOMP - 230 pages, softcover, $13.95

Attune Your Body With Dao-In. With over 85 photographs, Master Ni clearly and meticulously guides us through the 49 Dao-In postures never shown before. This companion book complements and explains the Dao-In DVD.

#BDAOI - 144 pages, softcover, $16.95

Secrets of Self-Healing. Dr. Mao Shing Ni presents this landmark book on natural healing, combining the wisdom of thousands of years of Eastern tradition with the best of modern medicine. Learn to treat common ailments with foods and herbs, and balance your mind and body to create vitality, wellness and longevity.

#BSHEAL—576 pages, softcover. $16.95

Esoteric Tao Teh Ching. In-depth techniques for advanced spiritual benefit. Master Ni's elucidated version of Lao Tzu's teaching will help us attain a deeper understanding of the ancient wisdom of the Tao Teh Ching. Presented as received from the teachings passed down for many generations, Master Ni has provided future generations with a precious bridge to the Subtle Truth.

#BESOT - 172 pages, softcover, $13.95

Golden Message. A summation of the teachings of Master Hua-Ching Ni by his sons. Find your own Golden Message by applying yourselves to gold, diamond, crystal, pearl, and jade self-study and correspondence courses. Learn how to become a student, how to become a teacher, and how to become a follower of The Integral Way.

#BGOLD - 141 pages, softcover, $11.95

Nurture Your Spirits. Master Ni presents the truth about spirits taken from his own personal experiences. What do Mantras, past lives, soul parties, ogres, channeling, spirits and ghosts have in common? What are their differences? Master Ni says that the truth can help us nurture our own personal spirits, the foundation of our being. Open your mind to consider a different reality in the spiritual realm.

#BNURT - 151 pages, softcover, $12.95

The Path of Constructive Life: Embracing Heaven's Heart . Remarkably simple, this work gives fresh direction and effective self-practices to achieve sexual harmony, emotional well-being, protection from harmful influences and a universal soul. An insightful guide to lasting health and positive inner development.

#BHEART—315 pages, softcover. $19.95

Internal Alchemy. In this book, Hua-Ching Ni reveals extensive information about internal energy transformation through captivating stories and straight answers to student questions. As he addresses alchemy, Hua-Ching Ni refers not to the immortality of the body but to the immortality of the spirit. He teaches the use of various aspects of this tradition so that spiritual students can attain genuine transformation.

#BALCH - 248 pages, softcover, $17.95

Life and Teachings of Two Immortals: Volume II. Born in 871 A.D., Chen Tuan lived joyfully in the Hua mountains. Every day he enjoyed the movement of the mountain breeze, the warmth of the sun and the brightness of the moon. He was famous for the foreknowledge he attained through deep study of the I Ching and his unique method of "sleeping cultivation." Includes details about microcosmic meditation and mystical instructions from the Mother of Li Mountain.

#BLIF2 - 167 pages, softcover, $12.95

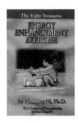

Eight Treasures: Energy Enhancement Exercise. Dr. Mao presents the Eight Treasures, combining toning and strengthening movements, stretching and specific breathing techniques. A must for all students and practitioners of energy disciplines and Oriental Medicine which can be practiced by anyone at nearly any age and fitness level. A companion to the Taoist Eight Treasures DVD.

#BEIGH - 202 pages, softcover, $17.95

Workbook for Spiritual Development - A practical, hands-on approach for those devoted to real spiritual achievement. Diagrams showing sitting and standing postures; even a sleeping cultivation. Plus an entire section of ancient invocations. One of our most important publications for our more advanced readers.

#BWORK - 212 pages, softcover, $14.95

Instructional DVDs for Learning Tai Chi and Qi Gong

Tai Chi Sword. A short instructional sword form to help sweep away emotional obstacles and enhance protective energy. Excellent for developing spiritual focus.

#DSWORD - 19 minutes, DVD, $24.95

18-Step Harmony Style Tai Chi with Dr. Mao Shing Ni. These easy-to-learn 18 movements form the basis of the 108-step Harmony Style Tai Chi form. Doing these 18 steps for a few moments every day can bring balance and gracefulness into your busy life. Tai chi also enhancea your vitality and strength.

#DSTEP—28 minutes, DVD, $24.95

Attune Your Body with Dao-In with Hua-Ching Ni. Dao-in is an ancient Taoist yoga that preceded tai chi and is practiced sitting and lying down. Despite its simplicity, it unlocks stagnant energy, increases strength and health, and calms the emotions. Includes self-massage and meditation.

#DDAOI—50 minutes, DVD, $24.95

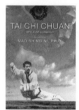

Tai Chi Chuan - Style of Harmony. This program presents Harmony style, which refines the energy from the food we eat and the air we breathe and transforms it into Jing, or physical essence. The gentle fluid movements of this style reflect the nature of harmony itself.

#DTAISET - 98 minutes, 2 DVDs, $29.95

Cosmic Tour Ba Gua. This style of movement has healing powers similar to Tai Chi, but the energy flow is quite different. Ba-Gua consists of a special kind of walking which corrects the imbalance and disorder of "having a head heavier than the rest of the body." Walking in a large circle over an open ground with the image of a flying bird or a swimming fish, Cosmic Tour reduces the congestion of our modern, intellectual lives and brings the energy down to the feet in order to improve circulation.

#DCOSM - 55 minutes, DVD, $24.95

Tai Chi Chuan: The Gentle Path. The movements of this exercise guide us to follow the gentle, cyclical motion of the universe. By gathering energy in the lower *tan tien*, the root center, the movements will change our internal energy and guide us to a peaceful and balanced life.

#DGENP - 45 minutes, DVD, $29.95

Taoist Eight Treasures. Thirty-two gentle, non-impact exercises unique to the Ni family facilitate energy flow and strengthen vitality. Combining stretching, toning and strengthening movements, the exercises are named for various aspects of nature such as ""Great Birds Spreads its Wings"" and ""The Weeping Willow Shivers in the Early Morning Breeze"."

#DEIGH - 46 minutes, DVD, $24.95.

Tai Chi Chuan: An Appreciation. Hua-Ching Ni displays "Gentle Path," "Sky Journey," and "Infinite Expansion" in an uninterrupted format. All three Taoist esoteric styles have been handed down by highly achieved masters.

#VAPPR - 30 minutes, DVD, $29.95

CDs for Calming, Releasing and Centering

Meditation for Stress Release with Dr. Mao Shing Ni. Are you suffering from tension and anxiety? This body/mind qi gong meditation can bring you calming relief. Beginning with the guiding words of Dr. Mao, you can use awareness and visualization to find relaxation, tranquility and a restored spirit.

#DSTRESS—26 minutes, CD, $12.95

Invocations for Health, Longevity and Healing a Broken Heart with Dr. Mao Shing Ni. Thinking is louder than thunder! Repeating these three magnificent Chinese invocations can help you achieve physical, emotional and spiritual health. The lush tones of the words are believed to have unique powers of their own. These invocations are an inheritance from ancient China that are finally translated into English.

#CDINVO—23 minutes, CD, $12.95

Meditations to Live to be 100 with Dr. Mao Shing Ni. This guided meditation leads you through the cornerstone practices for building vital life energy, including rejuvenating and cleansing meditations, visualization, hand postures, and breathing plus lifestyle and diet tips.

#CDLON—2 hours, 2 CDs, $19.95

OTHER RESOURCES FROM THE NI FAMILY

Tao of Wellness, Inc.

1131 Wilshire Boulevard, Suite 300

Santa Monica, CA 90401

310-917-2200

www.taoofwellness.com

The Tao of Wellness Center for Traditional Chinese Medicine provides services to foster the integral way to total well-being and a long life. Each patient is seen as an individual whose health is immediately affected by his or her lifestyle including diet, habits, emotions, attitude, and environment. The center, co-founded by Drs. Daoshing and Mao Shing Ni, focuses on acupuncture and Chinese herbs for complete health, longevity, and fertility.

Wellness Newsletter:

View it and subscribe online at *www.taoofwellness.com*

Tao of Wellness Magazine:

Free subscription. Email name and address to: *info@taostar.com*

The Wellness Store

1412 Fourteenth Street

Santa Monica, CA 90404

310-260-0013

www.wellnesslivingstore.com

order@taostar.com

Herbs, books, tai chi and qi gong classes; healthy living products; public lectures; art gallery.

The Tao Store

www.taostore.com

info@taostar.com

800-772-0222

This is an online store that features products from the Tao of Wellness, Traditions of Tao, and SevenStar Communications. It includes herbs, nutritional supplements, books, DVDs, and CDs that relate to natural health, chinese medicine, Taoist movement arts, and the Integral Way of Life Tradition.

Yo San University of Traditional Chinese Medicine

13315 W. Washington Boulevard, 2nd floor

Los Angeles, CA 90066

877-967-2648; 310-577-3000

www.yosan.edu

One of the finest and most academically rigorous Traditional Chinese Medical schools in the United States, Yo San University offers a fully accredited Master's degree program in acupuncture, herbology, tui na body work, and chi movement arts. In this program, students explore their spiritual growth as an integral part of learning the healing arts.

Yo San University Bookstore

13315 W. Washington Boulevard, Suite 200

Los Angeles, CA 90066

310-302-1207

www.taostar.com

taostar@taostar.com

A complete traditional Chinese medical university bookstore with a selection of Western medical books, acupuncture supplies and herbal supplements from a Chinese pharmacopeia passed down through 38 generations. Also available are tai chi and chi gong DVDs, meditation CDs to relieve stress, heal a broken heart or manage pain, books on Taoist teachings that nurture the spirit, and tools for positive living.

Yo San University Clinic

Low-cost academic clinic where patients are treated by supervised interns. Licensed acupuncturists also available.

Yo San University Fertility Center

Consultation and treatments are given by doctoral-level acupuncturists who are doing residency in the nation's first ever Doctoral Program in Reproductive Medicine and Infertility (REI).

College of Tao & Integral Health

Taoist Studies

Intro to Taoist Spiritual Development Course

info@taostudies.com

www.taostar.com

People who have read one or more books on the Integral Way of Life will find support in this study program. Having deepened their understanding and experience of the Way, students will learn how to live a constructive path of life.

Integral Health Studies - Traditional Chinese Medicine (TCM)

Includes CD, classroom notes, and all course materials

800-772-0222

taostar@taostar.com

www.collegeoftao.org

Listen to actual classroom lectures by exceptional teachers while having classroom notes for your home study. May include reading and journal assignments, charts, textbooks, or raw herbs. Courses include:

Chinese Herbology

Traditional Chinese Medicine Theory: I, II, III

Chinese Acupuncture Points

Becoming a TCM Healer - 14 CEU credits

The Power of Natural Healing - 14 CEU credits

Essence of Five Elements - 7 CEU credits

Concepts of Chinese Nutrition - 15 to 45 CEU credits

Please contact us for updates and a brochure.

Chi Health Institute

PO Box 2035

Santa Monica, California 90406-2035

310-577-3031 (voicemail)

www.chihealth.org

The Chi Health Institute (CHI) offers professional education and certification in the Ni family *chi* movement arts including tai chi, chi gong, and Taoist meditation.

InfiniChi Institute International

PO Box 26712

San Jose, CA 95159-6712

408-295-5911

www.longevity-center.com/infinichi/infinichi.html

(or do a search for InfiniChi Institute International)

Professional training in *chi* healing leads to certification as an InfiniChi practitioner. The program is designed to develop your energetic healing abilities utilizing the Ni family books and texts that relate to Traditional Chinese Medicine, chi gong, Chinese bodywork, and natural spirituality. It features a progressive, systematic program that nurtures understanding, facilitates skill development, and promotes self-growth.

Integral Way Community Website

PO Box 1530

Santa Monica, CA 90406-1530

310-577-3031 (voicemail)

info@taostar.com

www.integralway.org

Learn about natural spiritual teachings as transmitted by the Ni family through books, mentoring, and retreats organized by the mentors of the Integral Way. The Integral Way Community (a.k.a. Universal Society of the Integral Way) assists people in achieving physical, mental, spiritual, moral and financial health by nurturing self-respect and by offering methods of self-improvement based on the principles in the classic works of the *I Ching* and Lao Tzu's *Tao Teh Ching*.

Acupuncture.com

www.acupuncture.com

800-772-0222

info@taostar.com

Acupuncture.com is the gateway to Chinese medicine, health, and wellness. From this site you can purchase Tao of Wellness herbal products, choose from a large selection of traditional formulas, and buy acupuncture books and related products.